Motivating Learning

Motivating Learning

Jill Hadfield and Zoltán Dörnyei

PEARSON

Harlow, England • London • New York • Boston • San Francisco • Toronto • Sydney • Auckland • Singapore • Hong Kong
Tokyo • Seoul • Taipei • New Delhi • Cape Town • São Paulo • Mexico City • Madrid • Amsterdam • Munich • Paris • Milan

Pearson Education Limited
Edinburgh Gate
Harlow CM20 2JE
United Kingdom
Tel: +44 (0)1279 623623
Fax: +44 (0)1279 431059
Web: www.pearson.com/uk

First published 2013 (print and electronic)

The rights of Jill Hadfield and Zoltán Dörnyei to be identified as authors of this work has been asserted by them in accordance with the Copyright, Designs and Patents Act 1988.

Pearson Education is not responsible for the content of third-party internet sites.

ISBN: 978-1-4082-4970-3 (print)
 978-0-273-78612-2 (eText)
 978-0-273-78617-7 (pdf)

British Library Cataloguing-in-Publication Data
A catalogue record for the print edition is available from the British Library

Library of Congress Cataloging-in-Publication Data
Hadfield, Jill, author.
 Motivating learning / Jill Hadfield and Zoltan Dornyei.
 pages cm
 Includes bibliographical references.
 ISBN 978-1-4082-4970-3
 1. Language and languages–Study and teaching. 2. Language teachers–Training of.
3. Motivation in education. 4. Curriculum planning. I. Dörnyei, Zoltán, author. II. Title.
 P53.85.H33 2013
 418.0071--dc23
                                                        2012045534

10 9 8 7 6 5 4 3 2 1
16 15 14 13

Illustrations by Phil Burrows
Cover image © Getty Images

Print edition typeset in 10/13pt Scene Std by 35
Print edition printed and bound in Malaysia (CTP-VVP)

NOTE THAT ANY PAGE CROSS REFERENCES REFER TO THE PRINT EDITION

Contents

Preface

About the series

Research and Resources in Language Teaching is a ground-breaking series whose aim is to integrate the latest research in language teaching and learning with innovative classroom practice. The books are written by a partnership of writers, who combine research and materials writing skills and experience. Books in the series offer accessible accounts of current research on a particular topic, linked to a wide range of practical and immediately useable classroom activities. Using the series, language educators will be able both to connect research findings directly to their everyday practice through imaginative and practical communicative tasks and to realise the research potential of such tasks in the classroom. We believe the series represents a new departure in language education publishing, bringing together the twin perspectives of research and materials writing, illustrating how research and practice can be combined to provide practical and useable activities for classroom teachers and at the same time encouraging researchers to draw on a body of activities that can guide further research.

About the books

All the books in the series follow the same organisational principle:

Part I: From Research to Implications

Part I contains an account of current research on the topic in question and outlines its implications for classroom practice.

Part II: From Implications to Application

Part II focuses on transforming research outcomes into classroom practice by means of practical, immediately useable activities. Short introductions signpost the path from research into practice.

Part III: From Application to Implementation

Part III contains methodological suggestions for how the activities in Part II could be used in the classroom, for example, different ways in which they could be integrated into the syllabus or applied to different teaching contexts.

Part IV: From Implementation to Research

Part IV returns to research with suggestions for professional development projects and action research, often directly based on the materials in the book. Each book as a whole thus completes the cycle: research into practice and practice back into research.

About this book

All educators will know that motivation is a vital element in learning. In fact motivation, or the lack of it, is the most commonly cited explanation for success or failure in language learning. This book presents a new theory of motivation based on a vision of the Ideal Future L2 Self. If students have a rich and inspiring vision of the language learner they could become, it argues, they will be motivated to work hard to actualise the vision and become that learner. The book explores how the various components of the theory could be structured into a teaching sequence. It offers a variety of imaginative classroom activities designed to go from creation of the initial vision of the L2 Self to actualisation of the vision through goal setting, task identification, selection of appropriate learning strategies and time management. Activities have both motivation building and language learning aims so that teachers can use them in a variety of ways. The book offers suggestions for selecting activities according to teaching context to design a 'motivational programme', and for integrating such a programme into the language syllabus. Finally it presents ideas for using the activities in the book as a basis for action research.

We hope that you will find the series exciting and above all valuable to your practice and research in language education!

Chris Candlin (Series General Adviser) and
Jill Hadfield (Series Editor)

Publisher's acknowledgement

The publishers are grateful to Sean Morey for permission to reproduce The Mom Song in Activity 23.

Part I

From research to implications

Motivation and the vision of knowing a second language

Language teachers frequently use the term 'motivation' when they describe successful or unsuccessful learners. This reflects our intuitive belief that during the lengthy and often tedious process of mastering a foreign/second language (L2), the learner's enthusiasm, commitment and persistence are key determinants of success or failure. Indeed, in the vast majority of cases learners with sufficient motivation *can* achieve a working knowledge of an L2, *regardless of* their language aptitude, whereas without sufficient motivation even the brightest learners are unlikely to persist long enough to attain any really useful language.

If motivation is such a crucial feature of successful learning, teacher skills in *motivating* learners should be seen as central to teaching effectiveness. Indeed, research has shown that for many teachers problems about motivating pupils are the second most serious source of difficulty (after maintaining classroom discipline), preceding other obviously important issues such as the effective use of different teaching methods or a knowledge of the subject matter. If you have ever tried to teach a language class with reluctant, lethargic or uncooperative students, you will know from bitter personal experience that researchers got it right this time!

Since the mid-1990s there have been some publications specifically discussing various techniques and strategies to motivate language learners, and in 2001 Zoltán produced a summary of this practical knowledge in his book *Motivational strategies in the language classroom*. This collection showed that there is much more to motivational strategies than offering rewards and punishment (i.e. 'carrot and stick') and drew attention to a rather unexplored area of teacher development. In our book we present a new approach to conceptualising motivation – centred around the learner's *vision* – that complements the techniques that were presented in the 2001 book. This approach originates in psychology, and has been adapted for use with language learners in Zoltán's recent motivation theory, the 'L2 Motivational Self System' (Dörnyei, 2005, 2009). The material in this book is an attempt to put the theory to the test by putting it into practice! Drawing on Jill's extensive experience in teacher education and materials writing, we have set out to develop classroom material that is practical and yet fully compatible with the latest theoretical insights. In the rest of this introduction we offer an outline of the L2 Motivational Self System with the aim of creating a context for the activities in the following chapters. More detailed explanations and illustrations of the various components will be offered in the later chapters, and in Part IV we also provide guidelines on how to undertake practice-based research in the classroom.

Motivation and the self

The L2 Motivational Self System is rooted in 'self research' in psychology. In 1986 Markus and Nurius published in the journal *American Psychologist* an important paper that was simply entitled 'Possible selves' (Markus and Nurius, 1986), and since then the concept of the possible selves has made a remarkable career. It refers to the future-oriented aspect of our self-concept, describing our visions of what we *might* become, what we *would like to* become, and what we are *afraid of* becoming. When we use the word 'vision', we use it literally: possible selves are more than mere long-term goals or future plans in that they involve tangible *images* and *senses*. If we have a well-developed possible future self, we can imagine this self in vivid, realistic situations. A good example of this imagery aspect is how athletes regularly imagine themselves completing races or stepping onto the winning podium in order to increase their motivation. That is, possible selves are a *reality* for the individual: people can 'see' and 'hear' a possible self.

Ideal selves, ought-to selves and the L2 Motivational Self System

From the point of view of education, one type of possible self, the *ideal self*, appears to be a particularly useful concept, referring to the characteristics that someone would ideally like to possess. It includes our hopes, aspirations and wishes – that is, our dreams.

It requires little justification that if someone has a powerful ideal self – for example a student envisions him/herself as a successful businessman or scholar – this self-image can have considerable motivational power, because we would like to bridge the gap between our actual and ideal selves. This is expressed in everyday speech when we talk about someone following or living up to his or her dreams.

A complementary self-guide that has educational relevance is the *ought-to self*, referring to the attributes that one believes one ought to possess. It is therefore linked to our sense of personal or social duties, obligations or responsibilities. This self-image is particularly salient in some Asian countries, for example, where students are often motivated to perform well to fulfil some family obligation or to bring honour to the family's name.

These two future self-guides are highly useful for understanding the motivation to learn a foreign language, and therefore Zoltán has included them as two key components in his theory:

- *Ideal L2 Self*, which concerns the L2-specific facet of one's *ideal self*: if the person we would like to become speaks an L2, we can speak about an 'ideal L2 self', which is a powerful motivator to reduce the language gap between our actual and ideal selves.

- *Ought-to L2 Self*, which concerns L2-related attributes that one believes one *ought to* possess to avoid possible negative outcomes (e.g. letting down parents or failing an exam), and which therefore may bear little resemblance to the person's own desires or wishes.

Of course, in an ideal case the ideal and the ought-to L2 selves – that is, what we want to do and what we think we should do – coincide!

The L2 Motivational Self System also includes a third component, which is directly related not to future selves but rather to the influence of the students' learning environment:

- *L2 Learning Experience*, which concerns situation-specific motives related to the immediate learning environment and experience (e.g. the positive impact of success or the enjoyable quality of a language course).

The inclusion of this third component was motivated by the recognition that the various facets of the classroom learning situation, such as the teacher, the curriculum and the learner group, also have a major motivational impact on the learners. Indeed, for some language learners the initial motivation to learn a language comes not from internally or externally generated self-images but rather from successful engagement with the actual language learning process, for example because they discover that they are good at it. As the saying goes, success breeds success!

Thus, to sum up, the L2 Motivational Self System suggests that there are three primary sources of the motivation to learn a foreign/second language: the learner's vision of her/himself as an effective L2 speaker, the social pressure coming from the learner's environment and positive learning experiences.

Conditions for the motivating capacity of vision

Past research has shown that the motivational capacity of one's vision – that is, future self-guides – is not automatic; it becomes an effective motivator only if some conditions are in place:

- The learner *does have* a desired future self-image: not everyone is expected to possess a developed ideal or ought-to self-guide.

- The future self-image is *elaborate* and *vivid*: a possible self with insufficient specificity and detail may not be able to evoke the necessary motivation.

- The future self-image is perceived as *plausible*: possible selves need to be perceived as *possible*, otherwise they remain at the level of sheer fantasy. Yet, they cannot be perceived as comfortably certain either, or else the learner will not feel pressed to exert effort.

- The future self-image *does not clash* with the expectations of the learner's family, peers and other elements of the social environment (cf. the detrimental group norm of 'language learning is girly').

- The future self-image is *regularly activated* in the learner's working self-concept through various reminders.

- The future self-image is accompanied by relevant and effective *procedural strategies* that act as a *roadmap* towards the goal; even if an athlete manages to enthuse him/herself by envisaging success, he/she will need a training plan and a coach to channel the released energies onto a productive path.

- A desired future self-image is offset by a counteracting *feared possible self* in the same domain; that is, failing to reach the possible self has negative consequences.

Becoming aware of these conditions is of great significance, because we genuinely believe that, if these conditions are met, motivation arises automatically and powerfully. Therefore, the central idea in motivating language learners from a vision perspective is to create the above conditions. This book has been written to show you and your learners how.

A visionary motivational programme

Our specific motivational programme rests on the assumption that a particularly effective way of motivating learners is to enable them to create an *attractive vision* of their future language self. This motivational programme consists of six components:

- *Creating the vision:* The first step in a motivational intervention that follows the self approach is to encourage learners to construct their Ideal L2 Self – that is, to *create an L2-related vision*. The term 'constructing' the Ideal L2 Self is, in fact, not entirely accurate because it is highly unlikely that any motivational intervention will lead a student to generate an ideal self out of nothing; the realistic process is more likely to involve *awareness raising* about and *guided selection* from the multiple aspirations, dreams, desires, etc. that the student has already entertained in the past, while also presenting some powerful role models to illustrate potential future selves.

- *Strengthening the vision:* Methods of imagery enhancement have been explored in several areas of psychological, educational and sport research in the past, and the techniques of *creative* or *guided imagery* can be utilised to promote Ideal L2 Self images.

- *Substantiating the vision:* Effective visions share a mixture of imagination and reality and therefore, in order to go beyond mere fantasising, learners need to anchor their future self-guides in a sense of realistic expectations. This substantiating process requires honest and down-to-earth reality checks as well as considering any potential obstacles and difficulties that might stand in the way of realising the vision.

- *Operationalising the vision:* Future self-guides need to come as part of a 'package' consisting of an imagery component *and* a repertoire of appropriate plans, scripts and specific learning strategies. This is clearly an area where L2 motivation research and language teaching methodology overlap.

- *Keeping the vision alive:* 'Warmers' and other classroom activities can all be turned into effective ways of reminding students of their vision and thus to keep the enthusiasts going and the less-than-enthusiasts thinking.

- *Counterbalancing the vision:* We do something because we want to do it *and also* because not doing it would lead to undesired results. Regular reminders of the limitations of not knowing foreign languages as well as highlighting the duties and obligations the learners have committed themselves to as part of their ought-to selves help to counterbalance the vision with a feared self.

How this book is structured

The central section of the book is Part II (From implications to application), as this contains a wide range of hands-on classroom activities with ongoing commentary that highlights the process of the journey from research to practice. This part is further divided into three chapters and several sections, following the main components of the L2 Motivational Self System set out in Part I.

Part III (From application to implementation) offers suggestions and discussion on integrating the activities into a language syllabus, on how to make the activities workable in different classrooms and contexts and on how to use the activity types as models to generate further activities.

Finally, Part IV (From implementation to research) is to encourage teachers to develop the ideas in the book in terms of research and teaching in the practice of their own classrooms. We offer there sources for further reading and ideas for exploring and extending the theme of motivation and the ideal self through conducting 'action research' in the language classroom. Have fun!

Part II
From implications to application

Content selection

Part II, the central section of the book, contains a wide range of practical classroom activities directly derived from the theory of the L2 Motivational Self System. As we saw in Part I, this theory has three 'pillars': the Ideal L2 Self, the Ought-to L2 Self and the enjoyment of the L2 Learning Experience. It is clear that the third element is conceptualised on a different level from the other two: the Ideal L2 Self and the Ought-to L2 Self are both described as future self-guides, whereas the learning experience is external to the self and thus represents a different area of motivation. Furthermore, the impact of the learning environment concerns such a huge area – for example, curriculum, choice of activities, teacher roles and attitudes, group dynamics – that we felt that it would be difficult to translate this into a meaningful selection of ready-to-use activities. These considerations led to the decision that the bulk of the material in this book (in Part II) will focus on the ideal and ought-to self-guides, and the motivational impact of the learning experience will be discussed only briefly and in a more discursive manner in Part III.

The visionary motivational programme outlined in Part I includes six steps:

- Creating the vision
- Strengthening the vision
- Substantiating the vision
- Operationalising the vision
- Keeping the vision alive
- Counterbalancing the vision

All these steps are primarily concerned with creating an ideal self-image, with relatively little said about ought-to self images. This is fine, but there is one element of the ought-to self that we would like to emphasise, the need for it to be aligned with the ideal self (after all, if our heart and our mind pull us in different directions, that can't be productive). We therefore added a seventh step: 'Unifying the vision' by aligning the future selves.

Sequencing

The ordering of the components in the original programme was not explicitly designed to reflect an actual teaching sequence. Therefore we have made some sequencing decisions to achieve what we see as a logical flow of the steps.

- First, the Creating, Strengthening, Substantiating and Counterbalancing steps can all be seen as part of a broader process of building up the vision, while the Operationalising and Keeping the Vision Alive steps involve parallel processes that take place after the initial generation of the vision.

- Secondly, although creating the vision would undoubtedly be the first step, the vision needs substantiating – that is, be made subject to reality checks – before being enhanced and strengthened. Equally, counterbalancing the vision should not come last, since it involves envisioning failure; instead, the sequence, when translated into classroom reality, should end on an upbeat, not a potentially negative note.

Accordingly, the classroom motivational sequence moves from initial vision creation, through a number of reality checks, to test whether the vision of an Ideal L2 Self is in fact achievable in practice. Other self-guides – the feared self and the ought-to self – are then evoked as further motivational forces and finally work is done on strengthening and enhancing the vision, and making it more precisely targeted to appropriate real life and classroom situations. Once these initial steps are completed, two parallel processes succeed them: Mapping the Journey, which is concerned with operationalising the vision by providing a route map for actualising the self-guides, and Keeping the Vision Alive, which is concerned with providing lively classroom activities that will activate the ideal self (see Figure 1).

Imaging Identity: My Future L2 Self

- Creating the vision
- Substantiating the vision
- Counterbalancing the vision
- Unifying the vision
- Enhancing the vision

Mapping the Journey

- From vision to goals
- From goals to plans
- From plans to strategies
- From strategies to achievement

Keeping the Vision Alive

- Developing identity
  - Targeted visualisations
  - Role models
  - Self-belief
- Making it real
  - Simulations
  - Cultural events

Figure 1. Schematic representation of the sequencing of the motivational programme

Where to find out more

- *Identity and language learning:* Dörnyei and Ushioda (2009); Murray, Gao and Lamb (2011); Norton (2000); Pavlenko and Blackledge (2004)

- *Possible self theory:* Dunkel and Kerpelman (2006); Lee and Oyserman (2009); Markus and Nurius (1986); Oyserman and James (2009)

- *Self-discrepancy theory:* Higgins (1987)

- *The L2 Motivational Self System:* Dörnyei (2009); Henry (2010)

- *The role of the imagination and using visualisations:* Arnold, Puchta and Rinvolucri (2007); Berkovits (2005); Fezler (1989); Hall *et al.* (2006); Leuner, Horn and Klessman (1983); Markman, Klein and Suhr (2009); Singer (2006); Taylor *et al.* (1998); Dörnyei and Kubanyiova (in press)

- *Athletes and motivation:* Cumming and Ste-Marie (2001); Gould, Damarjian and Greenleaf (2002); Morris, Spittle and Watt (2005)

Chapter 1
Imaging identity: my future L2 self

In *The multilingual self*, Natasha Lvovich (1997: 8–9) writes, 'I could never travel to the country of my dreams to work, study, develop professionally, or see people who were dear to me.' Instead, she describes creating an imaginary French identity for herself, learning to speak with a Parisian accent, reading books in French, learning French songs, mastering numerous written genres, cooking French recipes and dipping 'the imagined croissant into coffee . . . A French personality, after all, was much less confusing and safer than being a Jew in Soviet Russia. It was a beautiful Me, the Me that I liked.'

Section 1: Creating the vision

What is meant by the vision of a future possible self?

The cornerstone of this new theory of motivation is the idea of the overall self not as something single, fixed and permanent but rather as the collection of a number of different, shifting and sometimes even contradictory selves.

Some of these selves exist in present reality: if you think of yourself in different situations, you may be able to identify, for example, a home self, a work self, a self who is a mother or father, a self who is a daughter or son, a self with one group of friends, a different self with another group of friends.

Other selves exist not in the present, but in an imagined future: if you think of yourself in the future, you may be able to identify a self that you feel you *should be*: a harder worker, a calmer parent, a more generous friend, a fitter self, for example. You may also be able to identify a self that you are *afraid of becoming* – a jobless self, a nagging self, a friendless self, an unhealthy self – or a self that you *would like to become:* the successful self, the popular self, the rich self, etc. These future selves have been called the Ought-to Self, the Feared Self and the Ideal Self.

In this section we are concerned with creating a vision of the Ideal L2 Self: the future identity that our learners envision for themselves as L2 speakers.

Why is it important to create a vision?

For most of us, there is an obvious discrepancy between the current/actual self and the ideal future self. Self-discrepancy theory states that people will be motivated to reduce this discrepancy so that their current self begins to approach their vision of their ideal self. Motivation thus consists of the desire to reduce the gap between present and ideal selves. In order for the discrepancy to be perceived and thus for this desire to exist, there will need to be some kind of a vision of what the ideal future self is.

Most people have some idea of an ideal future self, but this may not be substantial, elaborate or vivid enough to motivate them. It is important therefore to work on raising awareness of an individual's future desired self, on building up the image and making it as detailed and vivid an imagined reality as possible. The more detailed and vivid the vision, the more the ideal self will come to seem a possible future reality rather than a vaguely imagined dream, and the more the vision seems to be an achievable possible reality, the greater the motivation to strive to achieve it.

What does creating a vision entail?

We are dealing here with an imagined future, but one that the individual desires to become a reality. The role of the imagination will therefore be vital here, but – paradoxically – an imaginative experience that makes the future as concrete and as real as possible. We need to harness what Hazel Markus (2006) called 'the remarkable power of the imagination in human life' in order to create a future self state that is as real and tangible as possible.

What, therefore, is the aim of this section?

The aim of this section will be to provide activities that enable students to create, or build on, visions of their future possible selves that are:

(a) attractive and desirable,

(b) elaborate and detailed,

(c) vividly experienced: concrete and tangible.

How can this best be translated into practice in terms of usable classroom activities?

The technique that seems best to fulfil the above aims is the use of *visualisation*: the deliberate creation of a mental image (or series of mental images) according to a script or a series of instructions dictated by the teacher (or given by the learner to himself). Visualisation and mental imagery have been used in many disciplines, for example medicine and sport, to improve motivation, provide an impetus to goal setting and improve performance. In *The inner game of tennis*, for example, Timothy Gallwey (1972) directs the reader to 'take some time to imagine yourself hitting the ball with power, using the stroke which is natural to you. In your mind's eye, picture yourself serving, filling in as much visual and tactile detail as you can. Hear the sound at impact and see the ball speed toward the service court.' It is clear from this example that a visualisation needs to be precise and detailed, and needs to involve use of all senses in order to make the imagery as vivid as possible.

Visualisation has formed part of the L2 teacher's repertoire of techniques for some time, but has usually been used as a starting point for language work: the dictation of a visualisation of a story, landscape or dream sequence, for example, can lead into a speaking or writing activity. The visualisations of the future L2 self in this section can similarly lead into language work, but have the added aim of generating the vision of the future self necessary for motivation.

Does this involve any issues and problems?

Two immediate issues concern student response to visualisation. Although visualisation is an engaging activity that most students find interesting and enjoyable, there is a danger that they may become bored if this is the only activity type provided. Further, visualisation is obviously a technique that will work best with students with a visual learning style; students with other learning styles, in particular kinesthetic students, may find visualising harder to do.

Other issues involve privacy and permanence. Although the vision of a future possible self is an intensely personal and individual one, it does not follow that it should remain a private one. On the contrary, the vision will seem less of a daydream and more a possible reality if it is communicated to and validated by others. Finally, a visualisation is in essence transitory and intangible. There is a danger that even powerfully evoked visions can become lost or forgotten if not recorded in more permanent form.

How can these issues best be dealt with?

Although visualisation is necessarily the central element in this section, it is important to complement it with other activities partly for the sake of variety and to cater for different types of learner and different learning styles, and partly to add valuable other dimensions to the process of creating a vision.

Mime and *drama*, for example, offer another, more kinesthetic, way of envisioning a possible future reality and a way of extending the original vision and bringing it to life, as does *roleplay*, which allows students to enter into the imaginative world of the vision and give their ideal self a voice.

Mask making and *poster making* are similarly kinesthetic and provide an opportunity to express the vision through art rather than words, and, importantly, to record aspects of the vision in a more concrete permanent form than either visualisations or drama. *Photos* are also a way of making the vision concrete, tangible and permanent. All these artistic forms of expression lend themselves to classroom displays and thus provide both a permanent reminder and a public statement of the vision.

It also seemed important that private visions of the future possible self should come into the public arena and be shared with and validated by others in a different way: through group and pairwork retelling of the individual 'stories' of their visualisations. These shared stories can be written up afterwards in the form of stories, poems, letters or dialogues to preserve the vision in a more concrete, less ephemeral form. The creativity involved in these activities makes a powerful contribution to learners' sense of identity and self-worth.

How can I best use these activities in my classroom to achieve the aim of this section?

Which activities should I use first?

The activities in this section are in an order in which you could use them in the classroom, with more general activities such as envisioning a general future self coming before more precisely targeted visions, and visualisation activities coming before speaking or writing activities.

Do I need to use all the activities?

This is very much a 'pick and mix' research and resource book, rather than setting out an actual teaching sequence, and it is up to you to select activities that you and your students will enjoy and find meaningful.

How much time should I allocate to creating a vision with my learners?

This depends very much on the constraints of your timetable and curriculum. However, creating the initial guiding vision of an L2 identity is such a fundamental part of motivation that it may be worth allocating a lesson or two to this at the start of your course. Once the vision is firmly in place, you have two options: (a) Use the activities in subsequent sections as brief warm-up, 'reminder' or 'goal setting' activities, perhaps at the start or end of each week. (b) If you have more time, as each activity has a language and skills practice aim as well as a motivation aim, they can provide task-based language practice in the form of an ongoing 'identity project' – an integrated skills project that the students follow throughout the term, resulting in the creation of a tangible finished 'product': posters, displays, wikis or bebo pages, identity booklets, etc.

How should I select activities in this section?

Your aims in selecting activities for an introductory session should be to choose activities that will appeal to your class with the following aims in mind:

- to enable students to create a vivid and detailed vision of their future possible L2 identity
- to give students the opportunity to share their visions with each other
- to end up with a record of the visions in more permanent form.

What is the best way of conducting visualisation?

First get the students into a relaxed state. You could play some soft, gentle music, ask them to close their eyes and go through a relaxation exercise like the one in Activity 1. Get them to try and empty their minds of random thoughts, preoccupations and worries by focusing on their breathing. Then when they are relaxed and focused on the moment, begin by introducing some pleasant images to create a positive feeling. When giving script directions, speak calmly and slowly and pause between instructions for a few seconds to allow students to conjure up the images. It is a good idea to practise the script first so that you feel confident and relaxed.

Note: In Part III there is more advice on integrating activities into a course and adapting them to different levels and other contexts.

Activity 1: Future Alternatives

Aim: To provide examples of different Ideal L2 Selves

Level: Intermediate up

Time: 40 minutes

Materials: Reading texts and worksheet

Preparation: Make enough copies of each text for a quarter of the class. Make one copy of the worksheet for each student

Language practice	
Functions	future wishes
Skills	reading, speaking
Language areas	present simple, would like to, want to

Procedure

1. Divide students into four groups and give out different texts to each group. Give each student a worksheet.

2. Get them to work individually to complete Questions 1 and 2, then compare their answers with their group.

3. Get them to make brief notes to summarise their text.

4. Regroup the students to make new groups, each having four students who have all read different texts. The easiest way to do this is to give each student in each group a number: 1, 2, 3, 4, 5, etc. Then regroup them by saying 'All the ones from each group come and sit here, all the twos over here', and so on.

5. Get the students to roleplay being the writer of their text and to tell the others about their ideal future self.

6. Get them to discuss which vision, or parts of visions, are most like their own.

Worksheet 1

1. Look through the text quickly. Choose a title for the text:
   - My successful career self
   - My successful tourist self
   - My global citizen self
   - My member of the community self

2. Read again and choose the statements that the writer of your text might make:
   - I want to speak English (or any other target language) to communicate with people from different countries.
   - The foreign language is the key to a successful career for me.
   - I will enjoy my holiday more if I can speak the language.
   - I want to understand a different culture.
   - I want to earn a good salary and have an interesting job.
   - I want to be able to chat a little to local people about simple things.
   - I want to be able to understand TV and films in the language.
   - I want to be able to read fluently without spelling out.
   - I want to be able to communicate everywhere when I travel.
   - I want to feel a part of the society I live in.
   - I want to support a language that has been in danger of dying out.
   - I want to communicate with friends from other countries.

3. Make notes to summarise the text so that you can tell other people about it.

4. Get together with three other students who have read different texts. Imagine you are the writer of your text. Use your notes to tell the others about your 'vision' of your future self.

5. Discuss: Which of the four different visions is most like your own vision?

Texts

1   Summer's ideal future English self

I see myself in the future with a higher degree in English. After graduating, I apply for a job with an international company. The job is very interesting and has a good salary so there are a lot of applicants. However I am well-prepared and confident so I have no trouble speaking English at the interview. I see myself at the interview, answering all their questions confidently and fluently. After the interview, I feel I have done well, though I am nervous about the outcome. The next day, the phone rings. The Manager tells me I have been selected for the job. My first job will be in London and later I will be posted to Geneva. I really enjoy my career with this company, working in different countries with international colleagues and communicating in English in my work and daily life. I do well in my job and soon get promotion.

2   Charlie's ideal future Maori self

I see my future self fully prepared and confident, able to do a *noho* on a *marae*. I am standing in the *wharenui* giving my *mihi*, a fully rounded confident detailed *mihi*, and then later, after I sit down, listening and understanding the *te reo* Maori speakers giving theirs. I spend a weekend on a *marae* and can follow the conversations, speeches and stories. I see myself sitting at home, able to watch Maori TV programmes: documentaries, films, news. I can write letters and emails in *te reo*. I can play Maori songs on my (basic strums) guitar and know what the words mean, having memorised them. I can read descriptions in museums like *Te Papa*, understand the words in my NZ passport . . . read old documents. On a weekend or holiday, I pull up the car in somewhere like Kaeo and have no problem asking for directions and understanding the reply, and then make conversation with local people over a cup of tea or a beer in the pub. I can enjoy an evening in a bar talking with Maori locals about their place and local stories. I am currently halfway through a very dense coursebook, *Te Kakano*. In the same series are three more books. I envision myself completing the whole course taking me up to BA level . . . maybe even attending a graduation ceremony on the *Marae*. I want to be as rounded a New Zealander as possible, able to empathise with and understand the Maori dimension of this society. I want to feel I am doing the right thing socially and politically: Maori language has a small 'world' status (in terms of international communication) but within NZ it is 'equal' to English and this needs support and encouragement after a long decline and near death.

3   Kyoko's ideal future English self

I am interested in travelling and meeting people from other countries. Here in Kyoto I went to an International School so I have many friends from different countries and we use English to communicate no matter what country we come from. I like to speak English as much as possible. In the future I see myself talking to my friends in English when we meet or on Facebook and being able to express my ideas exactly. In the evenings, I watch English TV programmes, read English books or go to English movies and I am able to understand everything. I see myself in the future travelling round the world and maybe working in different countries. I am able to communicate with people and make friends everywhere I go.

4   Jill's ideal future Greek self

My imagined Future Self is on holiday in Greece. We have rented a car (managing all the paperwork in Greek) and are driving through a town in Greece and I can read all the street signs easily and fluently without spelling out the letters. We stop and park the car. I read the instructions on the meter and know how much to put in. I only have a note but I am able to ask someone for change for the meter. Next, we have to find the museum. The map is not clear so I ask a passerby for directions. Not only can she understand me – but I understand everything she says! We reach the museum and I buy a guide-book in Greek. I can read fluently and understand everything it tells me about the objects in the museum and their history. After the museum, we go for lunch in a little *taverna*. I can read the menu and order in Greek. When the meal comes, it is exactly what I thought I was ordering too! It's hot in the afternoon so we go back to the villa for a rest and then down to the beach. I read the newspaper on the beach. On the way back I do the shopping for supper and can ask for what I want, identify the labels on the packets, understand how much it comes to and chat a little to the shopkeeper about where we come from and what I'm cooking for supper. In the evening, the landlady invites us in for a drink and I can chat to her easily and fluently. We talk about families, different customs in Greece and England and politics. I even make a joke!

Activity 2: Introduction to Visualisation

Aim: To act as a generic introduction which can be used to create a relaxed atmosphere conducive to visualisation

Level: Elementary up

Time: 2–3 minutes

Materials: None necessary

Preparation: Rehearse the script

Language practice	
Functions	giving instructions
Skills	listening
Language areas	imperatives

Procedure

1. Begin by telling students that you are going to get them to relax and close their eyes – not to go to sleep, but to allow some images to come into their minds.

2. Play some quiet, soothing music to set the atmosphere if you like and then begin to dictate the script with instructions for relaxation. Allow time between each instruction for students to relax and follow the directions.

3. This introduction can lead into any of the visualisations in the chapter.

Script

Close your eyes . . . find a comfortable position . . . breathe deeply . . . take long breaths in . . . and out . . . try to direct your thoughts to what is happening here and now . . . in the room around you . . . be aware of sounds in the room around you . . . now be aware of how you are sitting . . . begin to relax . . . begin by relaxing your toes . . . your feet . . . they feel heavy now . . . now your legs . . . let them feel relaxed . . . now your body and your shoulders . . . drop your shoulders . . . your arms . . . your hands . . . now your neck . . . your head . . . your whole body is relaxed . . . now concentrate on your breathing . . . in . . . out . . .

Activity 3: My Ideal Self

Aim:	To introduce the students to the concept and image of a general ideal self
Level:	Elementary up
Time:	10–15 minutes
Materials:	None necessary, music if preferred
Preparation:	Rehearse the script

Language practice	
Functions	narrative
Skills	listening and speaking
Language areas	present simple, past simple, landscape vocabulary

Procedure

1. Play some gentle music if you like, and introduce the activity with a relaxation script like the one in Activity 2.

2. Begin to narrate the script, pausing between instructions to give learners time to visualise the scene and actions.

3. When you have finished, ask learners to open their eyes and to share their visualisation with another student.

4. Round off the activity by asking learners to say something about their ideal self to the group as a whole. At this point, if you like, you can ask learners to say what part speaking the L2 plays in their vision of a future ideal self.

5. Learners can follow up the activity by writing their ideal self visions.

Script

Imagine . . . relax and let the pictures come into your mind as I speak . . . you are walking through a forest . . . what are the trees like? what is the path like? . . . is it steep? muddy? rocky? . . . what can you see around you? . . . what can you hear? . . . what is the smell of the forest? . . . how do you feel, walking through the forest? . . . the path leads to a cave . . . you enter the cave . . . inside the cave is huge and echoing . . . at the end is a waterfall . . . you know that if you walk through the waterfall you can be transformed . . . you can become your future self . . . take a little time . . . what is on the other side of the waterfall? . . . what is the future self that you want to be? . . . now you are walking through the waterfall . . . you have walked through the waterfall . . . what can you see? . . . who is the self that is waiting for you there?

Activity 4: Portraits

Aim: To introduce the students to the concept and image of a general ideal self

Level: Pre-intermediate up

Time: 10–15 minutes

Materials: Some reproductions of portraits, music if preferred

Preparation: Rehearse the script

Language practice

Functions	description of places and people
Skills	listening and speaking
Language areas	present continuous, present simple, present perfect, adjectives for physical description

Procedure

1. Show the class a number of portraits of different people.

2. Ask them to discuss in pairs:

   - Who is the person?
   - What does she do for a living?
   - What kind of a house does she live in? Where is it?
   - Is she happy? Why?
   - How would you describe her character?
   - Would you like to know her?
   - What question would you like to ask her?

3. Ask students to close their eyes and read out the visualisation script.

4. When you have finished, ask them to open their eyes and discuss their imaginary future portrait with a partner.

5. Students can write descriptions of the future portraits.

Script

Imagine . . . some years ahead in the future . . . you are having your portrait painted by an artist . . . what would you like the painting to show about your future self? . . . how old are you? . . . what do you look like? . . . where is the picture being painted? . . . why have you chosen that place? . . . what do you do for a living? . . . you are happy with your life . . . what things make you happy about your life? . . . how does the painting show that you are happy? . . . what does the painting show about your ideal future character?

Activity 5: L2 Greetings

Aim: To act as an ice-breaker/warm-up activity, introducing the students to the 'feeling' of an L2 self

Level: Elementary up

Time: 5–10 minutes

Materials: None necessary

Preparation: Find a photo or video clip of people greeting each other in the culture of the L2 you are teaching (e.g. shaking hands, bowing, etc.)

Language practice	
Functions	greeting
Skills	speaking
Language areas	Hello, How are you? I'm fine, etc.

Procedure

1. Show the photo or play the video clip, and explain the greeting customs of the country whose language you are teaching.

2. Ask learners to imagine they are in the country.

3. Get them to stand up and move around the class, greeting each other.

4. For post-elementary learners you could add specific details (e.g. you meet an old friend you haven't seen for a long time, you greet your boss at work, etc).

Activity 6: My Future L2 Self

Aim: To introduce the concept of a future L2 self and to get students to visualise in general terms what their ideal L2 self would be

Level: Pre-intermediate up

Time: 20 minutes

Materials: None necessary, soft music optional

Preparation: Rehearse the script until you feel confident and fluent with it; adapt/add to it if you would like to make it more relevant to your learners

Language practice

Functions	physical description
Skills	listening, speaking, writing
Language areas	simple present, present continuous, 'wh' questions

Procedure

1. If you like, play some soft background music. Introduce the idea of a future L2 self. What would your students like to be able to do in the L2? How would they like to feel when speaking the L2?

2. Ask learners to close their eyes. Tell them you are going to ask them to imagine themselves in the future, speaking the L2.

3. Begin asking the questions from the script, allowing time between each question for learners to imagine themselves in the scenario you 'dictate'.

4. When you have finished, ask learners to open their eyes and share their vision with the person sitting next to them.

5. Round off the activity by asking each learner to say something to the group about their partner's vision.

6. Ask learners to write up their visualisation.

7. Collect these in and go through them, making notes on the common themes. Is it possible to identify what elements are shared by the group

and what elements are individual or idiosyncratic? What elements are feasible and what might be unachievable? What is feasible within the parameters of the course you are teaching? Identifying these issues will be useful when you come to the next section: 'Substantiating the vision'.

Script

Imagine yourself in the future. You have studied (L2) . . . and now you can speak it well.

Imagine yourself . . . how old are you? . . . what do you look like now? . . . where are you living? . . . what is your house like? . . . who lives with you? . . . what job are you doing? . . . why do you enjoy it? . . . what makes you happy about your life? . . .

How is (L2) . . . useful to you now? . . . what can you do in (L2) . . . ? . . . do you use it in your work? . . . do you use it to study? . . . do you have (L2) friends? . . . do you use it when you travel as a tourist? . . .

Imagine the one that is most important to you: work, study, friends, travel . . . now imagine yourself in that situation . . . where are you? . . . in an office, at a meeting, on the phone, with friends, in a university, in the foreign country? . . . in a café? . . . in a shop? . . . in the street? . . . at a station? . . . choose one . . . where are you? . . . what does the place look like? . . . what can you see around you? . . . how many people are there? . . . what do they look like? . . . what are they wearing? . . . what can you hear? . . . what are you doing? . . . what are you wearing? . . . you are speaking (L2) . . . to someone . . . who is it? . . . what do they look like? . . . imagine that you are speaking (L2) . . . very well . . . what are you talking about? . . . what kind of things can you say? . . . how do you feel talking (L2) . . . ? . . . how do people react to you?

Activity 7: Identity Tree

Aim:	To extend awareness of dimensions that an L2 self can add to the existing L1 identity
Level:	Pre-intermediate up
Time:	20 minutes
Materials:	Large sheets of paper, coloured pens, or coloured paper and glue for collage
Preparation:	Prepare enough materials for your class

Language practice	
Functions	describing past experiences, describing personality
Skills	listening, speaking, writing
Language areas	simple present, simple past, present perfect, adjectives for personality

Procedure

1. Ask learners to close their eyes.

2. 'Dictate' the visualisation script.

3. When you have finished, ask them to open their eyes and give out the materials.

4. Ask learners to create a poster of an identity tree, showing the aspects of their core self and the new branches that an L2 self might offer.

5. Now get the learners to add leaves to the branches representing more precise things they want to be able to do in the L2 (e.g. order a meal in a restaurant, have a job interview, write an academic essay etc).

6. You can display the tree posters in the classroom.

7. As the course progresses, learners can add leaves to their tree, showing the new things they have learned in the L2 and new aspects of their L2 identity.

Script

Imagine you are a tree . . . your roots go right down into the soil . . . what are your roots? . . . your family? . . . the place where you grew up? . . . your child-hood experiences? . . . what has your family given you . . . how has your family shaped who you are? . . . what has the place you grew up in given you? . . . can you think of things that happened in your childhood that made you into the person you are now? . . .

Now think about the trunk of the tree growing tall and strong . . . what is in your tree trunk? . . . what are the main qualities in your personality? . . . think of three words to describe yourself . . . now think of the branches of the tree . . . what are your branches? . . . they could be contradictory . . . you could be shy but friendly . . . you could be funny . . . but thoughtful . . . there is room in your tree for many different branches spreading in different directions . . .

Now think of some branches that could blossom into your foreign language identity . . . they could be different from your normal identity . . . you might be serious in your own language but jokey in the foreign language . . . or you might find you are more serious and thoughtful in the foreign language . . . think about the branches of the tree that can extend your personality in new ways . . .

Activity 8: The Self I Can Become

Aim: To extend awareness of dimensions that an L2 Self can add
                    to the existing L1 identity

Level   Pre-intermediate up

Time: 20 minutes

Materials: Cardboard or plastic masks (see outline mask), felt tip pens,
                    paint, glue and materials such as sequins, feathers, beads

Preparation: Prepare enough masks and materials for all your learners

Language practice	
Functions	describing actions, personality and feelings
Skills	listening, speaking, writing
Language areas	past simple, present simple, because, vocabulary for personality and feelings

Procedure

1. Give out a mask to each learner and make materials available at a central desk.

2. Ask learners to draw a line to divide the mask in two in any way they choose – straight, wavy, vertical, diagonal, etc.

3. Tell them that the two halves of the mask represent their L1 self and their L2 self.

4. Ask them to create a split mask representing their L1 and L2 selves. They can do this representationally with a collage of materials, or with words written on each side of the mask, or with a combination.

5. Put learners in groups to explain their masks to each other. Alternatively ask everyone to say a couple of sentences about their masks.

6. Ask them to write a brief description of the mask, and create a classroom display.

Section 2: Substantiating the vision: what is possible

What is meant by 'substantiating the vision'?

'Substantiating the vision' means subjecting the original vision of the ideal future self to a reality check to make sure it is plausible and realistically achievable.

Why is it important to substantiate the vision?

Even the most elaborate, detailed and intensely desired vision of an ideal future self will be meaningless if it is so unrealistic as to be unachievable. Any effective future self must be a *possible* self; therefore the point of imagining an ideal future self is not to indulge in idle fantasy but to construct a future *possible* reality that can be planned for and worked towards.

What does substantiating the vision entail?

It will entail analysis of the original vision in order to determine what parts of the vision are achievable and what is unrealistic. Often this will depend very much on what timeframe is involved, so it may also involve breaking down and prioritising goals into short-term and long-term goals.

What, therefore, is the aim of this section?

The aim of this section is for students to analyse and discuss critically their original visions in order to end up with a revised vision that is realistic and practically achievable.

How can this best be translated into practice in terms of usable classroom activities?

Based on the vision of a future possible self, Segal (2006) called motivation 'the social cognitive act of future planning combined with the equally human act of generating fantasy'. It is this fusion of the imaginative and the practical that makes this such a powerful theory. The fantasy generated in the previous section will here be subjected to more cognitive discussion and analysis, and whereas the previous section depended on imaginative and affective activities, here the focus will be on the cognitive and rational: discussions, categorising and ranking activities.

Does this involve any issues and problems?

Students may not be clear at the outset how to differentiate a realistic from an unrealistic vision. They may have very different visions of what is realistic, or cling to an unrealistic vision. While all students will be used to discussion and analysis in a school or academic environment, some students will work better if affect and imagination are engaged.

Finally, it is important that the activities do not discourage students or make them lose the inspiration generated by vision.

How can these issues best be dealt with?

If an example is given at the outset, students will have a clearer idea of what might differentiate a realistic from an unrealistic goal. The section begins with an authentic example of a learner of Greek's vision of what she hopes to achieve at evening class. Students are invited to say what they think is realistic in the timeframe, and then to compare their ideas with what the writer wrote about herself.

It is important for purposes of group unity to bring any differing views of what is realistic to a class consensus. If individual analyses are commented on by peers, discussed in groups and finally debated with the whole class, these differences can be aired and ironed out. Your role as the teacher/group leader is important here: you will know from previous experience of teaching the course/level and knowledge of the timeframe, what may or may not be achievable, so it is important to take an active part in these discussions.

Although it is important to provide a cognitive and analytic counterbalance to the imaginative fantasies generated in Section 1, there should be an opportunity for students who work better through affect to have available activities, and these have been provided in the form of roleplay.

Finally, it is important not to lose sight of the vision: but to return, not to the original vision, but to a restated form of it, taking account of insights gained during the activities in this section.

How can I best use these activities in my classroom to achieve the aim of this section?

It is probably a good idea to begin with the reading/discussion activity in Activity 9. This will contextualise and give background to any subsequent activities. It also gives students an opportunity to analyse what is realistic and unrealistic in a more detached and impersonal way than if their own ideals and aspirations are involved. This can then give them a tool to dissect their own ideas.

Thereafter, any of Activities 10–14 can be used, depending on your own and your students' preference, and the activities you used previously from Section 1: for example, if you used Activity 6 in Section 1, then Activity 10 or 11 might be more appropriate; if you used Activity 7, then Activity 13 follows on from this.

Whichever activities you use, it is important to round off with a reformulation of the original vision. Activity 14 is designed to do this.

Note: In Part III there is more advice on integrating activities into a course and adapting them to different levels and other contexts.

Activity 9: Reality Check 1

Aim: To provide an authentic example of substantiating the vision of the future L2 self

Level: Intermediate up

Time: 40 minutes

Materials: Reading text, worksheet

Preparation: Make copies of the 'Ideal Greek self' text from Activity 1, as well as the 'Reality check' text and worksheet below for each student in your class

Language practice	
Functions	giving opinions, predicting
Skills	reading, speaking
Language areas	I think that . . . , will, will/won't be able to

Procedure

1. Give each student a copy of the 'Ideal Greek self' text and Worksheet 1.

2. Ask students to do Question 1 and check their answers with a partner.

3. Then ask them to work individually on Question 2.

4. Get them to compare answers and discuss them with a partner.

5. Then give out copies of the 'Reality check' worksheet and get them to compare their ideas with the writer's.

Worksheet 1 – Jill's ideal Greek self

Read the description of Jill's ideal Greek self. Jill is studying Greek at evening classes – a single two-hour class a week. She began studying in September and plans to go to Greece in May.

1. Which of the following does Jill want to be able to do on her Greek holiday?

   - read novels
   - read the newspaper
   - ask for and understand directions
   - read instructions
   - buy train tickets
   - read street signs, notices and labels
   - go shopping
   - read a tourist guide
   - ask for travel information
   - give and exchange personal information, e.g. family, where she comes from, etc.
   - talk about culture and customs
   - talk about politics
   - make jokes
   - fill in paperwork for rental car
   - read a menu
   - order a meal

2. Read through the description again. Circle any statements you think are unrealistic, given the time she has available. Draw a box around statements you think should be achievable. Underline statements you think will be possible but difficult.

3. Talk to a partner and compare your ideas. Then compare them with Jill's own reality check. Do you agree?

Worksheet 2 – My ideal future Greek self: reality check

Easy to achieve	Possible, but more long-term	Very hard to achieve	Not really achievable (without much more time than I have)
• reading street signs • understanding instructions on the meter • asking the way • asking for change • reading a menu • ordering a meal • shopping • reading labels • chat a little about where we come from	• understanding directions • talking about family	• talking about customs	• paperwork for renting the car • reading a museum guide in Greek • talking about politics

Activity 10: Reality Check 2

Aim: To get students to substantiate their vision of the future L2 self

Level: Intermediate up

Time: 40 minutes

Materials: Worksheet, students' own descriptions of their ideal L2 selves

Preparation: Make two copies of the 'Reality check' worksheet for each student in your class

Language practice	
Functions	giving opinions, predicting
Skills	writing, speaking
Language areas	I think that . . . , will, will/won't be able to

Procedure

1. Get students to reread their own descriptions of their ideal selves.

2. Give out the 'Reality check' worksheet and get them to fill it in for themselves.

3. Then get students to exchange their descriptions with a partner and give out the second copy of the 'Reality check'.

4. Get them to carry out the 'Reality check' on their partner's ideal L2 self description.

5. Put them in pairs to compare ideas.

Worksheet 1 – My ideal future self: reality check

Look back at what you wrote about your Ideal self. Which situations and aims do you think are:

- easily achievable

- possible but more long-term goals

- very hard to achieve

- not really achievable (without much more time than you've got)?

Fill in the table:

Easy to achieve	Possible, but more long-term	Very hard to achieve	Not really achievable

Activity 11: Reality Consensus

Aim: To generate a group discussion about which aspects of the learners' vision of their L2 selves are possible/feasible/achievable

Level: Pre-intermediate up

Time: 20 minutes

Materials: Ranking activity sheet

Preparation: Use the written descriptions of the visualisation in Activity 6; prepare a list of statements based on what the learners have written (see examples below) and use these to make a ranking activity (see example below)

Language practice	
Functions	saying what is possible/impossible/unlikely, giving opinions, describing personality
Skills	reading, speaking
Language areas	modals: can, will; would like; language for stating opinions and describing personality

Procedure

1. Tell your learners that you have read through their descriptions and the next stage is to consider what is feasible/achievable in reality.

2. Hand out the ranking sheets and ask each learner to complete them individually.

3. Put learners in pairs and ask them to compare their answers.

4. Join pairs into fours and ask them to share their ideas.

5. Ask each group of four to report their ideas to the class.

6. Draw the discussion together by summarising their ideas and adding your own on what is feasible/achievable within the parameters of the course you are teaching.

Example ranking activity

Number each statement:

1. I can do this now.
2. I will be able to do this by the end of this course.
3. I would like to be able to do this in the future.
4. I will probably not be able to do this.
5. Not part of my future L2 self.

Example list of statements

My future L2 self can . . .

o speak French with perfect pronunciation
o speak fluently and without hesitating
o speak French with no mistakes
o make jokes in French
o go shopping in French
o understand the menu and order meals in a restaurant
o have conversations with French people about books and films
o have conversations about politics
o have simple personal and social conversations.

My future L2 self is . . .

o lively   o sociable
o witty   o happy
o serious   o confident
o playful   o relaxed
o talkative

A similar ranking activity for EAP students could include 'can do' criteria like:

- understand everything the lecturer says
- take good notes from lectures
- understand all the main points of my lectures
- read scientific articles in English without using a dictionary
- write essays with no grammar mistakes
- write clear essays with few mistakes
- give a presentation about my subject
- be understood when talking to English students and lecturers
- feel confident about contributing in seminars

Activity 12: Dream On!

Aim:	To roleplay a discussion between dreamer and realist in order to determine what parts of the L2 vision are feasible
Level:	Intermediate up
Time:	20–30 minutes
Materials:	Role cards (to be prepared by teacher)
Preparation:	This activity is designed to follow on from the previous activity, so this should be done in preparation. Adapt the example role cards to suit your course and copy them for each pair of students

Language practice

Functions	saying what is possible/impossible/unlikely, giving opinions
Skills	reading, speaking
Language areas	modals: can, will, would like; language for stating opinions

Procedure

1. Copy role cards for each pair of students.
2. Put students in pairs and give each pair a set of role cards.
3. Tell them that one of them (A) is a dreamer and one (B) is a realist.
4. A should begin by telling B what he wants to be able to do at the end of the course. B should convince A that he may have to adjust his aspirations a little!
5. Begin by putting all the As in pairs and get them to prepare their roles and think out what they might say. Put the Bs together in pairs and get them to prepare in a similar way.
6. When they have had enough preparation time, regroup them so that the original As and Bs are together. Get them to roleplay the discussion.
7. Then get them to reverse roles.

Example role cards

You are on a one-month course for pre-intermediate learners of Spanish. By the end of the course you expect to be able to speak Spanish fluently, with excellent pronunciation and with no mistakes. You want to be able to talk about all kinds of subjects with Spanish people – art, films, politics – and you expect you will be able to do this by the end of the course.

A is a pre-intermediate student doing a one-month course in Spanish.

Ask A about the course he/she is doing. Let him/her explain what he/she expects to be able to do at the end. As he/she talks, you will feel that he/she expects too much! Try to convince him/her (politely!) that this may be impossible and suggest what might be more realistic.

Activity 13: Leaf Rating

Aim: This activity follows on from the Identity Tree activity in Section 1 (Activity 7) and is aimed at getting students to substantiate that vision by prioritising future aims.

Level: Pre-intermediate up

Time: 20–30 minutes

Materials: Students' original identity trees

Preparation: Make sure students have their original identity tree drawings

Language practice	
Functions	giving opinions, predicting
Skills	speaking
Language areas	I think that . . . , will/won't

Procedure

1. Ask students to look at the leaves they drew on their identity tree representing their future aspirations. Get them to rate them on a numerical scale from 1 = easy to achieve to 5 = very hard to achieve.

2. When they have finished, ask them to compare their ideas in small groups.

3. Bring the activity into a class discussion: ask each group to report back to the class on which aims will be easy/more difficult/unrealistic. Summarise their ideas on the board or on a flip chart as they talk.

Activity 14: Vision Revision

Aim:	To get students to revisit the written record of the visualisations they made in Section 1 and revise them in the light of the reality check
Level:	Pre-intermediate up
Time:	20–30 minutes
Materials:	Their original written visualisations
Preparation:	Prepare copies or originals of the written visualisations from Section 1

Language practice

Functions	physical description
Skills	speaking, writing, redrafting
Language areas	simple present, present continuous

Procedure

1. Give students their original written visualisations from Activity 1.

2. Tell them that the activity will involve rewriting, based on the discussion you have all had about what is feasible/achievable.

3. Get them to look through their visualisation and underline items that need rethinking.

4. Ask them to swap with a partner and check their partner's ideas for revision.

5. Let them discuss the ideas.

6. Students rewrite their visualisations in the warm light of reality!

Section 3: Counterbalancing the vision

What is meant by 'counterbalancing the vision'?

'Counterbalancing the vision' means that the vision of the ideal self should be balanced against a consideration of what would happen if the desired self were not attained.

Why is it important to counterbalance the vision of the ideal self?

Psychologists have found that motivation consists of two tendencies: *approach* and *avoid*. You can probably recognise this in your everyday life; there are goals you want to attain (e.g. getting fit, getting promotion at work) and undesired outcomes you wish to avoid (e.g. becoming unhealthy, remaining on a lower salary). Envisioning the ideal future self is obviously an 'approach' tendency, since motivation consists of the desire to approach the goal. Considering what would happen if the desired self were not attained would employ the 'avoid' strategy since motivation would consist of the desire to avoid a negative outcome. Oyserman and Markus (1990) suggested that future self-guides are at their most powerful when they use both approach and avoid tendencies (for example, if you have a strong positive vision of yourself as fit and healthy coupled with a strong desire to avoid being unfit and flabby). However, our natural tendency is often to focus on the positive and turn to dire alternatives only when all else fails; that is, we often only use the 'avoid' strategy to motivate ourselves when we are actually in danger of failing, in which case it might be too late or might only serve to increase the panic we are in! It would seem therefore that a balanced consideration of possible negative outcomes at an earlier stage could provide stronger motivation.

What does counterbalancing the vision entail?

It would entail raising the possible consequences of not achieving the desired ideal self in order to frame the two poles of the approach–avoid stimulus.

What, therefore, is the aim of this section?

The aim of this section will be to provide an opportunity for students to consider the possible consequences of not achieving the desired outcome, and to raise awareness of what obstacles might stand in their way in order to provide an 'avoid motivation' complementary to the 'approach motivation' of visualising an ideal future self.

How can this best be translated into practice in terms of usable classroom activities?

It seems that this subject is best dealt with cognitively rather than affectively, through discussion and analysis rather than visualisation or other affective and imaginative activities. 'Failure' is an emotive subject and powerful affective activities such as visualisation may have a negative effect on self-esteem and may thus 'counterbalance' the ideal self a little too far!

Does this involve any issues and problems?

The whole focus of contemporary methodology is to focus on the positive, whereas in previous decades emphasis has been on the 'stick rather than carrot' approach. Although both research in psychology and anecdotes from our own experience may suggest that fear of the consequences of not doing an action may be an equally powerful motivating factor than the rewards of doing the action, teachers and students may well feel hesitant about confronting the subject of failure in the classroom.

There are a range of different personalities in any class with a range of levels of confidence. Some may have too little self-concept of failure, leading to not enough work and needing therefore a gentle reminder, while others may have a deep-rooted insecurity and thus need their self-esteem boosting with an accent on the positive. Some may lack persistence or may wish to avoid feeling a failure at any cost and this might lead them to choose abandoning the course instead of failing – doing no work might be a more self-acceptable excuse for what they fear is lack of ability. How can we be sure who we are addressing? You may feel you know your students well, but do you know each of them deeply enough to be sure of their reactions in each case?

We may do things as much, or even more, from fear of undesirable consequences as from striving for desired futures (e.g. we may work hard to finish an article because of fear of missing the deadline rather than a vision of seeing the article in print), but this motivation is usually self-activated, not conjured up for us by other people. Indeed when the reminders come from other people (nagging editors, gloomy doctors) they may appear as depressing and demotivating.

How can these issues best be dealt with?

If you feel very hesitant about embarking on the subject of possible failure, it may be best to avoid it altogether. However, it may be worth trying to approach the subject in a calm and unemotional manner at the beginning of the course, when perhaps some strategies could be put in place for avoiding failure rather than possibly resorting to crisis management at a later stage of the course.

Only you can gauge the needs of your students. You may find you need to individualise your approach; for example, there may be a couple of students in the class who need a gentle reminder that the path they are following is unlikely to lead to success, whereas others may be all too driven by the spectre of possible failure.

Reminding students of the work they need to do in order not to fail a course can have a counter-productive effect. No one likes to be nagged! For this reason, the reminder should be kept light and brief and move towards positive strategies for avoiding failure.

With these caveats in mind, it seems that a framework for counterbalancing the vision would involve:

- a brief consideration of the possibility of failure
- a diagnosis of what could lead to failure
- an analysis of how it could be put right (or what strategies would be helpful)
- an expression of confidence in the students' ability to persevere and triumph in the end.

Activities in this section thus include:

- readings and discussion of a range of other students' reflections on possible negative outcomes
- consideration of the possibility of not achieving the desired goal
- activities that aim to identify obstacles to learning that might impede progress to the ideal self
- activities that begin to outline a route towards positive outcomes and avoiding negative ones: these activities serve as an introduction to the self-motivating strategies which will be developed in the next chapter, 'Mapping the journey: from dream to reality'
- return to a positive and strengthened visualisation of the ideal L2 self.

As part of this process we have made a distinction between external obstacles to learning (which may include such things as lack of time, lack of ability, etc.) and internal obstacles (such as the tendency to distract oneself with irrelevant tasks, the tendency to procrastinate, etc.) – we have called the latter 'self barriers'.

How can I best use these activities in my classroom to achieve the aim of this section?

Your aim should be to begin with briefly counterbalancing the vision, then to move on to discussion and analysis of obstacles to learning which will lead to a positive way forward to the reactivation of a strengthened and more mature vision.

Note: In Part III there is more advice on integrating activities into a course and adapting them to different levels and other contexts.

Activity 15: What If . . . ?

Aim: To provide examples of the consequences of not learning a
language

Level: Intermediate up

Time: 45 minutes

Materials: Reading texts, worksheets

Preparation: Make enough copies of each text for a quarter of your class.
Make one copy of the worksheet for each student

Language practice	
Functions	describing fears and worries
Skills	reading, speaking
Language areas	present simple, be afraid of -ing.

Procedure

1. Divide students into three groups. Give out the copies of the three texts
so that each group gets a different text. Give out one copy of the worksheet to each student.

2. Ask students to skim quickly through the text and answer the questions
on Worksheet 1. Get them to compare answers with someone from the
same group.

3. Then ask them to read again in more detail and to answer the questions
on Worksheet 2. Again, get them to compare their answers.

4. Ask all students to take their text and questionnaire and stand up.
Get them to walk around the class, interviewing other students to match
people to statements and the answer question 3.

5. When they have finished, ask them to find two people who have different
texts from them and to sit down with them.

6. Ask them to discuss question 4 together.

1. Skim read

Worksheet 1

Read quickly through your text.

Is the writer afraid of

- being disappointed in him/her self?
- being a disappointment to others?
- both?

Are the consequences

- external: not being successful in a chosen career?
- internal: not achieving a personal goal?
- both?

Worksheet 2 Questionnaire

2. **Look at the questionnaire.** Which statements apply to the writer of your text? Tick the statements and write his/her name by the statement.

Who is afraid of . . . ?	Write the name here
• not getting a job in Australia	_____
• losing the way in a foreign country	_____
• getting a low-status job	_____
• not earning enough money	_____
• trying to speak and being lost for words	_____
• feeling a fool in public	_____
• feeling excluded	_____
• being unable to read	_____
• missing the opportunity to understand the culture	_____
• not having enough confidence to speak with foreigners	_____
• being a disappointment to her family	_____
• not feeling a part of the society he is living in	_____
• not knowing enough of the language to make international friends	_____
• not being able to cope with travel situations as a tourist	_____
• not being able to understand TV or films	_____

3. **Find someone who . . .** Take your text and the questionnaire and go round the class. Try to find a person to match each item from the questionnaire. Write their names on Worksheet 2.

4. **Discuss.** Sit with three other people who have different texts from you. Give a short summary of your text. Discuss: which statements are true for you? Could you add any statements of your own?

Texts

Summer: English

If I don't study hard enough, I won't get a good degree. I am afraid of being a disappointment to my family. They would feel they had wasted their money in sending me abroad to study. Because of poor results in my degree and because my English is not as good as it should be, I cannot find a good job in Australia. I might have to take a boring job with a low salary or go back to China to find a job. Either way I would feel unfulfilled and disappointed. If I have to take a job in China I am afraid I will lose the opportunity to practise my English and I will become bad at speaking. I will lose the opportunity to work with an international company, to travel and make friends in other countries.

Charlie: Maori

Nothing would 'happen' if I don't achieve my aims in learning Maori except that I will disappoint myself and face my own limitations as a language learner. It would also be embarrassing to be tongue-tied in a public situation like giving a speech on a *marae*, being completely unprepared, groping for words, not being able to find the words I want and ending up completely inarticulate. It would be very frustrating to spend the weekend on a *marae* if everything goes over my head and I cannot understand what is going on. It would be particularly hard when everyone laughs at a joke and I seem to be the only one who can't understand!

I would be unable to understand Maori TV, read in Maori, understand place names or talk to people, beyond giving simple greetings. Mostly I would feel I have missed an opportunity of getting to know another culture from the inside by exploring its language. I feel there is so much more I could and should understand about New Zealand history, culture, peoples and society and I would feel disappointed in myself for not having made the effort to integrate more with the society I am living in.

Jill: Greek

This is my Greek holiday nightmare: we are driving along the highway and see a sign at one of the exits. It takes me so long to decode that we are well past the turnoff before I realise it says Argos – the town we want to go to. We take the next turnoff, but I can't understand the sign which says that it is a No Exit road. Some time later we find this out and have to retrace our steps. In Argos we park the car and head off for the museum. We get thoroughly lost and when we ask for directions I cannot understand the reply. Hot and cross, we arrive at the museum and find that the only guidebook is in Greek – too difficult to understand. We feel rather frustrated since we are not getting as much from the visit as we could. Lunch follows in a *taverna*. I order kebabs – successfully I think – but when the meal arrives, it turns out to be fish! We get back to the car and find a parking ticket. I had not understood the sign which said Pay and Display. I do some shopping for dinner and get by, pointing to what I want, but when the shopkeeper tries to talk to me I cannot understand. In the evening the landlady of our holiday flat starts to chat but I cannot understand a word she says and end up just nodding and smiling inanely.

If I don't learn Greek, I would feel I had lost an opportunity to get the most out of my holiday and cannot understand the people and culture as well as if I could speak the language.

Activity 16: What Gets in the Way of Learning?

Aim: To provide authentic examples of different obstacles to learning

Level: Intermediate up

Time: 40 minutes

Materials: Reading texts, name list and worksheets

Preparation: Copy and cut up the 'self barriers' texts so that there is one for each student in the class; copy and cut up the name list so there is one name for each student in the class; make one copy of the worksheet for each student.

Language practice	
Functions	describing problems
Skills	reading, speaking
Language areas	present simple, should, not very good/bad at

Procedure

1. Give out the texts. Ask the students to read their texts and to think of an appropriate name to describe that self barrier.

2. Then give each student a name from the name list. Make sure that they get a different name from the description they have. For example, if a student has a text describing a shy and unconfident self, give him any name except 'the unconfident self'.

3. Ask students to stand up and go round the class describing their self barriers to others until they find someone who can give them a suitable name.

4. Then ask students to sit in groups of five: texts 1–5 together and texts 6–10 together. If there is a group left over with fewer than five members, get them to join other groups. Give each student a worksheet.

5. In their groups, each student describes her self barrier as described in the text. The others guess the name. Then they discuss which self barriers they recognise in themselves. They should take brief notes on their worksheets to help them in the next stage of the activity.

6. When they have finished, ask one student from each 1–5 group to go to a 6–10 group and one student from each 6–10 group to go to a 1–5 group.

7. They should share information about what they discussed.

Worksheet 1 – Self Barriers

1. List the self barriers here: write the name and a few words of description:

Name	✓

2. Tick the ones you recognise in yourself!

3. Compare your answers with the rest of your group.

Texts

Self barriers

1. My intentions are good but when I settle down to do some work, I get very easily distracted. I think of other things to do, such as answering my emails, tidying the room – even making myself a list of things to do!

2. I have a lot of work at the moment and can't cope with anything extra. I always feel short of time and under pressure!

3. I'm not very good at time management. I don't plan a regular time to work so I spend days without studying, then suddenly get in a panic and try to do it all at once. I know I could get more done if I were more efficient with time and planning.

4. I give up easily – for example, if there are too many words I don't know in a text I find it an effort to work them out or look them up in the dictionary.

5. I tend to take on too many projects. I enjoy them all but don't have enough time for them all and end up doing none of them properly. Too many things to do! Too little time to do them!

6. I'm very bad at getting down to work. I tend to put things off and tell myself I can do my work another time.

7. I'm terribly disorganised. I'm not systematic about making notes or keeping a vocabulary book, for example. So my work is in a mess and when I want to study I can never find anything!

8. I am not very confident – particularly at speaking. I am afraid people will not understand me or will make fun of my accent, so I tend to avoid speaking. I didn't do very well at school, so I tend to doubt my abilities. I don't have much self-esteem when it comes to studying!

9. I know I don't do enough work. I like having fun too much, I suppose. It's very easy for my friends to persuade me that I don't need to study and to go out for the evening instead. No willpower, that's my problem!

10. I know I should keep up my German – and one of the best ways to do this would be by reading books. But I find it hard to make the effort: it's so much easier to read German novels in English – stupid I know!

Name list

- the unconfident self

- the weak-willed/easily tempted self

- the procrastinator self

- the lazy self

- the over-committed self

- the distracted self

- the stressed self

- the inefficient self

- the easily discouraged self

- the disorganised/unsystematic self

Activity 17: Identifying the Self Barrier

Aim: To raise awareness of the self barriers to learning and progress

Level: Pre-intermediate up

Time: 20 minutes

Materials: None

Preparation: Adapt the example anecdote to reflect your own experience

Language practice	
Functions	describing past experiences, describing personality
Skills	listening, speaking
Language areas	past simple, modals: had to, might; adjectives for personality

Procedure

1. Tell learners that you are going to discuss what things get in the way of learning. Suggest to them that we often get in the way of our own learning. Tell them a personal anecdote based on the things that get in your way or distract you from completing a task – for example:

   Yesterday I had to finish writing (an article/some reports/an essay). It felt like hard work, so I avoided doing it for a while: I washed the dishes and put them away. Then I remembered I had to water the garden. I came back in and made a few telephone calls. Finally, I sat down at my desk . . . but thought I might as well check my emails first . . . an hour later I looked at the clock and got a shock – I finally opened that document and started work.

   Explain to the students that what you have here is a conflict in your self – the self who wants to work or who knows you should work faces some 'self barriers' acting as obstacles in the way.

2. Put learners in pairs and ask them to share experiences where they have found it hard to settle down to work. Get them to identify their typical self barriers.

3. Get learners to describe their self barrier to the group – compile a list of possible self barriers, for example:

   o   the unconfident self barrier

   o   the distracted self barrier

   o   the stuck self barrier

   o   the lazy self barrier

   o   the avoidant self barrier

   o   the rebellious self barrier

Activity 18: Meeting the Self Barrier

Aim: To raise awareness of the self barriers to learning

Level: Pre-intermediate up

Time: 20 minutes

Materials: None

Preparation: Adapt the visualisation scripts to make them suitable for your particular learners and rehearse them

Language practice	
Functions	argument, advice, excuses
Skills	listening, speaking
Language areas	present simple, modals: should, ought to, need to

Procedure

1. Tell the learners that they are going to imagine meeting their self barriers.
2. Ask them to close their eyes.
3. 'Dictate' the visualisation.
4. Ask learners to open their eyes.
5. Put learners in pairs. Ask one in each pair to be a self barrier and one to be an ideal self. Get them to roleplay an argument that they might have. Then get them to reverse roles.
6. Ask any willing pairs to enact their argument for the class.
7. Collect suggestions from the ideal selves for arguments they could use to defeat the self barrier.

Script

Imagine . . . you have some language work to do . . . maybe you have to learn some vocabulary . . . maybe you have to write an essay . . . decide what the task is . . .

You are at home . . . visualise your room . . . where are you standing? . . . what can you see? . . . is the room tidy or untidy? . . . what temperature is it? . . . are you cold or hot – or comfortable? . . . what can you hear from the rest of the house? . . . from outside? . . . you know you have to do your homework . . . but you don't want to get down to it . . . your ideal self tells you to do your homework . . . your self barrier starts to find other things for you to do . . . what are they? . . . what does your self barrier tell you? . . . your ideal self replies . . .

How does it convince your self barrier to start the task?

Activity 19: Filmshots

Aim:	To dramatise, make concrete and gain perspective on typical obstacles in the self that stand in the way of learning
Level:	Pre-intermediate up
Time:	20 minutes
Materials:	None
Preparation:	This activity follows on from Identifying the Self Barrier and Meeting the Self Barrier (Activities 17 and 18)

Language practice	
Functions	room description, argument, suggestions, excuses
Skills	listening, speaking
Language areas	present simple, modals: should, ought to, need to, let's, shall we; how about, what about

Procedure

1. Introduce learners to the convention for writing a movie scene; for example:

   - summary description of setting: interior/exterior/place/time of day (e.g. INTERIOR: AUCKLAND: STUDENT FLAT: NIGHT)

   - a few lines of background information/more detail about setting (e.g. a room in student digs. Posters on the wall. Single bed in one corner. Table with laptop computer, piles of paper and remnants of takeaway meal and half-finished bottle of beer. Mario sits at table, opens up laptop, looks at screen)

   - dialogue; for example:

     Ideal Self: OK . . . Let's start the essay . . .

     Self Barrier: Yeah . . . cool . . . but look, let's clear the meal away first . . .

2. Ask them to write a movie scene with a dialogue between the ideal self who wants to get on with the task, and the self barrier, who distracts, avoids or rebels.

3. Students can share and read movie scenes together.

4. This can be developed into performances – and videoed if you have the equipment and learners are enthusiastic.

Activity 20: Two Roads

Aim: To raise awareness of the role of the self-guides

Level: Intermediate up

Time: 40–45 minutes

Materials: Copy of Robert Frost's poem 'The road not taken' (obtainable online), photo, role cards

Preparation: Copy the poem for each student or copy and cut into strips for each pair of students; copy a set of role cards for each group of three; find a photo that illustrates the poem

Language practice	
Functions	landscape description, giving reasons, conditions, warnings
Skills	reading and speaking
Language areas	past simple, 1st conditional, present simple, will

Procedure

1. Show students the photo. Ask them which path they would take? Why? Pre-teach some essential vocabulary: diverged, fair, undergrowth, wear, sigh.

2. Give them the cut-up strips and ask them to rearrange them into the complete poem. It will help to tell them there are four 5-line verses and the rhyme scheme is ABAAB.

3. Go through, or give out a copy of, the complete poem.

4. Ask students to think of a time in their lives when two paths diverged for them: they had a difficult choice to make – perhaps in their studies, choice of school, choice of career, job opportunity, etc. Give them a moment to reflect on this and then ask them to tell a partner about it.

5. Now ask them to imagine themselves as Frost's traveller at a fork in the paths. One path is easier, level, smooth; the other is more difficult, rocky, overgrown, steep and winding – but ultimately leads to a mountain top with stunning views, while the other comes full circle back to the starting place.

6. Put students in threes and give them each a role card. Give them some time to prepare and then ask them to argue it out, with the guides trying to convince the traveller to take their path.

7. When they have finished, ask for feedback on decisions and reasons for the decisions. Ask them to relate it to (a) the life situation they discussed earlier: which road was which for them and what decision did they make? (b) their future possible selves: how could they relate this to decisions about their future self?

Worksheet 1 – Role cards

A: Traveller

You are walking in the woods and have come to a fork in the path. You haven't got a map, so don't know which path to take. You meet two people and ask them for advice.

B: Guide 1 – self barrier

You have seen both paths – there is a level, smooth path that takes a nice easy circular route through the forest. You would recommend that one . . . it involves very little effort and is very pleasant. Plus you end up exactly where you started – so you know where you are: no effort, no danger of getting lost! Think up more reasons for taking the easy path and some for not taking the more difficult path.

C: Guide 2 – ideal self

You know both paths well. There is an easy one which isn't really all that exciting – takes you through the forest on a broad level track. It doesn't really go anywhere new – you just see more trees and at the end you are right back where you started. The other path is really exciting, though more challenging – steep and rocky and a long hard slog but at the end you come out on a mountain top with some inspiring views. Think up some more reasons for taking this path instead of the easier path.

Activity 21: Overcoming Obstacles

Aim: To introduce the students to some strategies for overcoming barriers

Level: Intermediate up

Time: 40–45 minutes

Materials: Copy of the strategies texts and worksheet

Preparation: Copy and cut up the texts so that there is one strategy for each student in the class; copy the worksheet so there is one for each student in the class

Language practice

Functions	describing habits
Skills	reading and speaking
Language areas	zero conditional, present simple

Procedure

1. Give out the texts. Ask the students to read their texts and decide which heading it comes under on the worksheet.

2. Ask students to stand up and go round the class describing their motivating strategy to others. When they hear about someone's strategy, they should make notes on it under the appropriate heading.

3. Then ask students to sit in groups of four/five to discuss which strategies would work for them and which they use already, and to think of some new ones they could add.

4. Ask each group to report back to the class.

5. You can collect the worksheets in and make a large poster incorporating all the suggestions, for classroom display.

Texts

Before I start work I try to visualise my goal, for example finishing my essay or learning 20 words – this motivates me to work hard.

I promise myself a reward or treat for when I finish the work – chocolate works well!

I have a strict routine for getting started on work: I find I tend to put off start-ing work, so I write down what time I am going to start and then I do a short simple task for 5–10 minutes, like learning five words. I find that if I can make a start with a very short task then it is easier to keep going.

I have worked out what distracts me and have a list of DOS and DON'TS on my wall, like 'DON'T answer emails till you have done one hour's work!' or 'Have a coffee when you finish the task, not in the middle!'

I try to find things to do to make the activity more fun, like making vocabu-lary learning into a game.

I get bored if I am doing one thing for too long so I plan my work in short blocks with a complete break in between where I get some fresh air or do some exercise – that helps me to stay fresh.

I listen to relaxing music – it makes me feel calm and happy.

I do a relaxation exercise before I start: it helps me to stop feeling stressed.

I have told my friends I am behind in my work because I go out too much – so now they make sure I am up to date with my work before they invite me out!

I don't find much time for learning verbs – so I have put posters up round the house – that way I see them often and I can learn a little bit at odd times of the day.

Worksheet 1 Strategies mindmap

Visualise a goal, e.g.:

Make rules, e.g.:

Break the task down, e.g.:

STRATEGIES

Make use of your environment, e.g.:

Develop a routine, e.g.:

Promise yourself a reward, e.g.:

Make it fun, e.g.:

Section 4: Unifying the vision

What is meant by 'unifying the vision'?

This chapter deals with the second main type of future self-guide identified by Higgins (1987) and Markus and Nurius (1986): the 'ought-to self'. This is defined by Markus and Nurius as 'an image of self held by another' and by Higgins as the representation of attributes that one believes one ought to possess – that is, obligations and duties that form *someone else's* vision of how the individual ought to behave. This could be the vision held by parents, family, teachers, peer group or society in general. Our ought-to self probably derives from a composite of all of these. An important condition for the effectiveness of future self-guides is that they should feel congruent with important social identities, that is, that the ideal and the ought-to selves should be in harmony. Accordingly, unifying the vision means working through the process of bringing the vision of the ideal self into harmony with the ought-to self.

Why is it important to do this?

It is important to do this so that the selves are not in conflict and to identify helpful insights that the ought-to self can offer (for example about study habits and behaviour) to aid in progress to actualising the ideal self.

What does 'unifying the vision' entail?

It entails, first of all, raising awareness of what an ought-to self is in general and exploring some of the complexities inherent in its make-up and our complex reactions to it. Then it will involve exploring what an ought-to L2 self could be and what aspects of this are in harmony with the ideal self. Finally, it will look at the ought-to self as enabler.

What, therefore, is the aim of this section?

The aim of this section is for students to identify those aspects of the ought-to self which will help them to realise their Ideal L2 Self.

How can this best be translated into practice in terms of usable classroom activities?

Both general and L2 ought-to selves can be evoked through visualisation. It seems important to give examples of other people's ought-to selves through reading and listening activities to make the concept more concrete. There-after activities can be both cognitive (e.g. discussions and questionnaires to enable students to analyse what is the best L2 ought-to behaviour and then to make learning resolutions for themselves) and affective (e.g. letter and dia-logue writing, poster making, fairytale creation) in order to develop a positive image of the ought-to self as a wise and helpful self-guide and enabling force.

Does this involve any issues and problems?

The main issue with the ought-to self is the contradictory and complex feelings we have towards it. Oscillating between helpful ally and nagging authority figure, it often seems to be pointing an accusing finger at us and making us aware of our shortcomings, rather than providing helpful strategies towards achieving our goals.

How can these issues best be dealt with?

Through raising students' awareness of how the ought-to self can be an enabling force, helping them achieve their goals, and creating more positive feelings towards it.

How can I best use these activities in my classroom to achieve the aim of this section?

Begin with an activity (e.g. numbers 22 and 23) to introduce the general idea of an ought-to self, and then follow this up with a discussion on the kinds of things an ought-to L2 self expects or the kind of advice it might give (num-bers 24, 25 and 26). Round off with an activity that presents the ought-to self as a wise and helpful ally to inspire positive feelings (numbers 27, 28 and 29).

Activity 22: Introducing the Ought-to Self

Aim: To introduce the concept of an ought-to self

Level: Pre-intermediate up

Time: 20 minutes

Materials: None

Preparation: Rehearse the script

Language practice	
Functions	description of people, daily routines, advice and suggestions
Skills	listening, speaking
Language areas	present simple, modals: should, ought to, would

Procedure

1. If you like, play some soft background music. Introduce the idea of an ought-to self: ask learners what an ought-to self does? What kind of things does it say to you?

2. Ask learners to close their eyes. Tell them you are going to ask them to imagine their ought-to self.

3. Begin asking the questions from the script, allowing time between each question for learners to imagine themselves in the scenario you 'dictate'.

4. When you have finished, ask learners to open their eyes and tell their partners about their ought-to self.

5. Round off the activity by asking each learner to say something to the group about the partner's vision.

Script

In your life you have some people telling you what you should do, what is good behaviour and bad behaviour . . . who are these people? . . . they could be parents, teachers . . . bosses at work . . . friends . . . doctors . . . TV . . . magazines.

Who are these people in your life? . . . what do they tell you? . . . what do your grandparents tell you? . . . teachers? . . . bosses? . . . friends?

As a result of these ideas from outside, you build an 'ought-to self'. This is the self that gives you advice and tells you what you should be doing. It is the voice in your mind that says, *'You should do this . . . No you shouldn't be doing this . . . You ought to do this instead . . .'.*

What kind of things does your ought-to self say to you? . . . are there some things it says very often? . . . what things do you listen to? . . . what things do you ignore? . . . if you could imagine your ought-to self as a person, what would he or she look like? . . . how would he/she dress? . . . imagine a perfect day for your ought-to self . . . what time would he/she get up? . . . what would he/she eat? . . . drink? . . . how would he/she interact with people? . . . what activities would he/she do? . . .

Imagine your ought-to language learning self . . . how would he/she behave in class? . . . spend his/her free time? . . . what work would he/she do out of class?

Activity 23: The Mom Song

Aim: To develop the concept of an ought-to self

Level: Intermediate up

Time: 40 minutes

Materials: The Mom Song (www.youtube.com)

Preparation: Watch the song and make a note of any vocabulary your students will need help with; copy the Ought-To Self Poem and the poem framework for each pair of students

Language practice	
Functions	commands, description of habits and behaviour
Skills	listening, speaking
Language areas	present simple, imperatives

Procedure

1. Put students in pairs to discuss what kind of things their parents told them to do when they were children or teenagers.

2. Preteach any vocabulary from the song that students may not recognise.

3. Listen to the Mom Song with your class. Use a version with subtitles.

4. Put students in pairs or groups to discuss what instructions they recognise from their own childhood – or if they are parents, what phrases they recognise in themselves.

5. Let them read the following two verses of *My Ought-to Self*, based on the beginning of the Mom Song.

   My ought-to self
   Is neat and tidy,
   Combs her hair,
   Wears sensible clothes
   And never skirts that are too short.

My ought-to self
Gets up early,
Eats a sensible breakfast,
Remembers appointments
And never forgets her homework.

6. Show them the pattern of the poem:

My ought-to self
_____s _____,
_____s _____,
_____s _____
And never _____.

7. Play the Mom Song again in sections. Pause after each section and ask students in pairs or groups to write the next verse.

8. At the end, ask pairs or groups to read their verses.

9. Ask individual students to write an Ought-to Self poem about themselves.

10. Get them to compare their poems in groups.

11. This activity can lead into the next activity (which also uses the Mom Song).

Activity 24: The Ought-to Self Song

Aim: To identify typical things the ought-to L2 self might say

Level: Intermediate up

Time: 40 minutes

Materials: The Mom Song (www.youtube.com)

Preparation: Copy the songlines worksheet for each student

Language practice	
Functions	commands
Skills	listening, writing, speaking (singing)
Language areas	imperatives, will, if

Procedure

1. Use steps 1–3 from Activity 23 if you have not already done Activity 23.

2. Play the Mom Song with your students and get them to try to sing along, hum or clap the rhythm of the first five lines:

    Get up now, get up now
    Get out of bed
    Wash your face
    Brush your teeth
    Comb your sleepy head

3. Give out the worksheet. Ask each student to choose lines from each of the five columns to make the first verse of an L2 Ought-to Self Song. Remind them that lines 2 and 5 should rhyme.

4. Put students in groups of three or four and get them to put their verses together to make a complete song.

5. If you think your students are capable, ask them to add a fifth verse.

6. Groups can perform their version of the song.

Worksheet 1 Songlines

Line 1	Line 2	Lines 3 and 4	Line 5
Sit down, sit down Hurry up, hurry up Speak up, speak up Get it done, get it done	And get your pen Sit at your desk And don't be late And don't be shy	Get your books Get your bag Take your pen Start your work Do your work Learn these words You can speak You can talk	I'll count to ten Don't make me wait Do your very best If you really try

Activity 25: Great Expectations

Aim: To identify L2 learning expectations

Level: Intermediate up

Time: 20 minutes

Materials: Questionnaire

Preparation: Copy the questionnaire for each student

Language practice	
Functions	discussing expectations and obligations
Skills	reading, speaking
Language areas	present simple, modals: should, ought to; expect to +infinitive

Procedure

1. Give a copy of the questionnaire to each student and ask them to complete it – they can tick more than one person for each item if needed. They can add items to the list.

2. Put students in pairs and ask them to discuss their answers.

3. Get the students to work in pairs and discuss:
   - what they do
   - what they don't do
   - what they ought to do

4. Get each student to decide on three things to do that would really help with their learning. Ask them to write them in the form of resolutions ('I will . . .') on a piece of paper and then to copy it onto another piece. They should keep one piece of paper and give the other to their partner to keep in a safe place.

5. You can periodically ask students to team up with their 'resolution buddy' and check up on how far their ought-to self is aligned with what they actually do.

6. You can collect suggestions from the whole class and make a poster of my ought-to L2 self.

Worksheet 1 Who expects you to . . . ?

Who expects you to . . . ?	Me	My parents	My teacher	My class-mates
• come to class on time				
• do your homework on time				
• study hard for exams				
• spend time learning vocabulary				
• spend time learning grammar rules				
• schedule time for revision				
• speak the L2 in class				
• listen in class				
• concentrate in class				
• listen or read the L2 outside class				
• do the best you can				
• _____				
• _____				
• _____				
• _____				

Activity 26: Advice From the Ought-to Self

Aim: To provide authentic examples of advice the ought-to self could give

Level: Intermediate up

Time: 40 minutes

Materials: Reading texts and worksheets

Preparation: Make one copy of the worksheets for each student; make one copy of the 'Greek self barrier' and 'Advice from the ought-to self' texts for each student; make enough copies of each of the 'Three self barriers' texts for a third of the class; you will need large sheets of paper and coloured pens for the posters.

Language practice	
Functions	describing problems and giving advice
Skills	reading, speaking
Language areas	present simple, should, ought to, imperatives

Procedure

1. Give students copies of the 'Greek self barrier' text and Worksheet 1.

2. Get them to do Question 1 individually, then put them in pairs to discuss Question 2.

3. Now give out the 'Advice from the ought-to self' text.

4. Get them to do Question 3 individually, identifying which self barriers each paragraph is addressed to. Then put them in pairs to compare the advice they thought of giving with the advice in the text.

5. Put students into three evenly sized groups. Give each a different text (Group 1: Text A; Group 2: Text B; Group 3: Text C). Give each student a name list.

6. Ask them to read the text individually and identify the self barriers from the list. Then ask them to jot down some advice from the ought-to self for overcoming those barriers.

7. Then get them to share ideas in the group.

8. Regroup the students into threes so there is one member from each group in the new group of three. The easiest way to do this is to give everyone in each group a number. Then say, 'All the ones sit here, all the twos over here', etc.

9. Get each student to tell the other two about the self barriers described in his/her text and the advice he/she would offer for overcoming those barriers. The others should contribute ideas of their own.

10. Get each group to make an 'Advice from the ought-to self' poster, outlining problems and offering advice.

Sample poster

Do you give up too easily when a task seems hard?

Make easy-to-keep contracts with yourself, like:

I will read for 10 minutes. During that time I will look up all the words in the dictionary and list them on vocabulary cards.

Worksheet 1 My learning Greek self barrier

1. Read the description of the difficulties Jill finds in getting down to study-ing Greek. Name the self barriers from the list below.

    - the stressed self barrier
    - the distracted self barrier
    - the inefficient self barrier
    - the easily discouraged self barrier

2. Discuss with a partner: what advice could you give her?

Advice from the ought-to self

3. Now read the 'Advice from the ought-to self' text. Fill in the names of the self barriers.

4. Discuss with a partner: Is the advice similar to the advice you would give?

Texts My learning Greek self barriers

I've been learning Greek at evening class for about six months now. I started well, but now I feel I'm not making much progress. These are my self barriers:

The _____ self barrier

I mean to put in the time at home studying – learning vocab, practising reading, etc., but whenever I settle down to do some work, I get very easily distracted. I think of other things to do, such as doing the gardening, a phone call I have to make, housework . . . the list is endless!

The _____ self barrier

I always feel short of time! Too much work! Too many things to do!

The _____ self barrier

I am very bad at scheduling a regular time to work so I forget to study, then suddenly need to do everything at the last minute. I wish I was better at time management and forward planning: I'd get a lot more done if I was more efficient!

The _____ self barrier

I give up easily. Reading Greek is hard because it's a different alphabet so I get tired of spelling out the words and if there are too many words I don't know in a text, I find it an effort to look them up in the dictionary.

Texts Advice from the ought-to self

What would the ought-to self say to these self barriers?

Your _____ **self barrier:**

This is probably a combination of really having little time but also of not organising the time you have well.

- Try to see Greek as a relaxation not more work. Maybe it's the place you work in: if it's at a desk, then it feels like work. Sit in an armchair, work in the garden, go to a café!

- Make use of 'dead time' – listen to recordings in the car, look at vocabulary cards at the bus stop, put up vocab lists on the fridge and label household objects so that you can be learning without setting special time aside.

Your _____ **self barrier:**

Plan to work for a shorter period. Tell yourself you will do all the distracting things at the end of the work period. Reward yourself by allowing a distracting activity at regular intervals – but only when you've done some work. You will probably find you don't really want to do the activity!

Your _____ **self barrier:**

Plan in very short regular times for study, e.g. 10–15 minutes a day rather than a guilty hour once a fortnight!

Your _____ **self barrier:**

Again, make an easy-to-keep to contract with yourself, like:

'I will read some Greek for 10 minutes. During that time I will look up all words in the dictionary and list them on vocabulary cards. Later in the day I will spend 10 minutes reviewing the words.'

Worksheet 2 Three self barriers

1. Read the text and choose two titles from the list to label the Problem Self that the writer describes:

   - the unconfident self barrier
   - the easily tempted self barrier
   - the procrastinator self barrier
   - the lazy self barrier
   - the over-committed self barrier
   - the disorganised self barrier

2. In your group, discuss what advice the ought-to self would give the writer. Make a list of your suggestions.

Texts Three self barriers

A. John: Italian

I decided I'd learn Italian at evening class this year. I enjoy the classes when I get to them, but I haven't been learning that much. The rest of the class seem to have got ahead of me. I know I should study in my own time but I have some problems with that:

- One problem is I have a lot of hobbies. I enjoy them all but don't have enough time for them all and end up doing none of them properly. Too many things to do! Too little time to do them!

- Another problem is I'm terribly disorganised. I'm not systematic about making notes or keeping a vocabulary book for example. So my work is in a mess and when I want to study I can never find anything!

B. Suzanne: Chinese

I am working in China on a two-year contract so I'm trying to learn some Chinese to communicate with people in everyday situations.

My biggest problem is that I am not very confident at speaking. I am afraid people will not understand me or will make fun of my accent, so I tend to avoid speaking. I'm not very musical and Chinese has tones – so I am always afraid I will get the wrong tone.

Part of it is shyness, but if I'm honest I think part of it is laziness: if things are an effort, like sitting and learning vocab or making myself have a go at speaking, I try to avoid them, because it's easier.

C. Jung Chang: English

I'm studying English at university in Australia. Last week I got the results of my mid-year exams and my grades weren't very good. I got a bit of a shock!

I know I don't do enough work. I like having fun too much I suppose. It's very easy for my friends to persuade me that I don't need to study and to go out for the evening instead. I haven't got much willpower so I give into temptation easily.

Even if I stay home, I'm very bad at getting down to work. I tend to put things off and tell myself I can do my work another time.

Activity 27: Making Friends with the Ought-to Self

Aim: To create a positive image of the ought-to self

Level: Intermediate up

Time: 40 minutes

Materials: Speech bubble poster

Preparation: Copy the speech bubble poster for each group of 6–8 students

Language practice	
Functions	describing past experience and feelings, giving advice
Skills	speaking, writing
Language areas	past simple, present perfect, modals: should, ought to

Procedure

1. Introduce the topic: we are going to think about people we admire; people in life who have inspired us or been a role model. Ask students individually to think about the following question: In your life who has inspired you?

2. Put them in pairs to discuss this question.

3. Then ask them: Did those people have anything in common?

4. Give students some individual reflection time for the following question: Think of your vision of your future possible self. What do you think those people might advise you to do to achieve this vision?

5. Get the pairs to discuss this and compare ideas.

6. When the pairs have discussed this, group the pairs in fours to discuss these ideas.

7. Then ask them to put together these pieces of advice in a list of suggestions.

8. Group the fours in eights and ask them to put all the advice together and choose the four or five most useful/inspiring pieces of advice.

9. As a group, imagine your role model/friend is giving you this advice and fill in the speech bubbles on the poster.

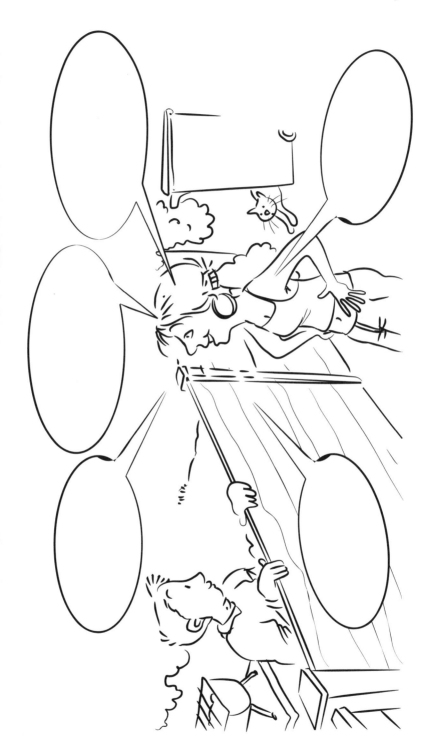

Activity 28: Meeting the Mentor

Aim:	To build the idea of an ought-to self as a wise and helpful self-guide
Level:	Elementary up
Time:	15–20 minutes
Materials:	Pictures, fairytale, music if preferred
Preparation:	Rehearse the script

Language practice

Functions	narrative, description
Skills	listening and speaking, writing in follow-up activity
Language areas	present simple, past simple, vocabulary for describing relationships and people

Procedure

1. Read the fairytale with the students.

2. Introduce the idea that in many myths, fairytales and quest stories there is a wise figure who offers advice. The advice will guide the hero/heroine onto the right path and help him/her achieve the goal. The advice is not always easy to follow, however!

3. The wise figure comes in many forms – often an old woman, sometimes a mysterious cloaked figure who offers cryptic advice . . . sometimes in unlikely forms such as a beggar, an animal, a tree.

4. Ask students to close their eyes and 'dictate' to them the visualisation.

5. When you have finished, ask them to open their eyes and discuss their image of the mentor with a partner.

6. Then ask them to close their eyes again, and 'dictate' the second part of the visualisation.

7. Ask them to open their eyes and share the advice their mentor gave them.

Script, Part 1

Close your eyes . . . imagine . . . you are walking down a path in the middle of a dark forest . . . imagine the forest . . . it is damp and misty . . . the path is overgrown . . . the trees are dark and tall, shutting out the light . . . the forest is very silent . . . just occasional bird calls through the mist . . .

You are lost and do not know where to go . . . all you know is there is a long way to go . . . suddenly, out of the mist you see a shadowy figure . . . some-how, although the figure is vague and mysterious you know it can help you . . . what does this figure look like? . . . a woman? . . . a man? . . . an animal? . . . how old? . . . what is it wearing? . . . let the picture come clear in your mind and then turn and tell your partner.

Script, Part 2:

You approach the figure . . . and ask for help . . . what do you want to know? . . . what advice are you given? . . .

You continue along the path following the advice . . . and suddenly you are out of the wood . . . you have entered a meadow full of flowers . . . birds are singing . . . the sun is shining . . . you can see the path ahead winding up a mountain . . . you know it will not be easy, but now you can see where to go . . .

Let the picture come clear in your mind and then tell your partner. When you have told each other about the visions, try and say what it might mean in terms of your own life – problems you are facing, advice you might need, directions you might take . . .

Activity 29: The Fourth Man

Aim:	To raise interest in the concept of self-guides
Level:	Intermediate up
Time:	30 minutes
Materials:	Text
Preparation:	Copy one text for each group of 4–5 students; cut it up so that there are three sections: (a) Paragraph 1, (b) Paragraph 2, (c) Paragraphs 3 and 4

Language practice	
Functions	narrative, description
Skills	reading, discussion
Language areas	present simple, past simple, past perfect

Procedure

1. Ask students to brainstorm real-life heroes/heroines who have found themselves in difficult or extreme circumstances (e.g. Hillary on the ascent to Everest, Florence Nightingale, Amundsen on expedition to South Pole, Lindbergh on first transatlantic flight, Reinhold Messner on first ascent of Everest without oxygen, Yuri Gagarin or Neil Armstrong on space voyage).

2. Ask them:
   - What was the hero/heroine's ideal self and feared self?
   - What could be the self barriers?
   - What kept them going?

3. Divide students into groups of 4–5. Give each group the first paragraph of the text. Ask them to discuss what the 'Third Man Factor' could be.

4. Give half of each group the second paragraph of the text and the other half the third and fourth paragraphs. Get them to read and to transfer the information.

5. Ask the groups to discuss – in what ways is the 'Third Man' like an ought-to self?

Worksheet 1 The Third Man Factor

A phenomenon known to psychologists as the 'Third Man Factor' often occurs to people who find themselves in extreme or dangerous conditions: climbers, Polar explorers, divers, solo sailors.

The most famous of these experiences is Ernest Shackleton's account of a mysterious 'Fourth Man' who joined him and his companions on their journey through the waters of the Southern Ocean and across the mountains of Antarctica. Their ship had become trapped in Antarctic ice, a thousand miles from human habitation. They lived on the ship for ten months but it was gradually crushed by the ice. Shackleton led his men on a five-month journey in small boats and then went on foot with two companions across a mountain range to reach a whaling station. He wrote later, 'Doing that long march of thirty-six hours over the unnamed mountains and glaciers of South Georgia, it seemed often to me that we were four, not three.' Each of his companions later confessed that they had experienced exactly the same thing.

This sense of a mysterious presence is well-documented. In his book *The third man factor*, John Geiger has collected dozens of stories, for example that of Di Francesco who was on the 84th floor of the World Trade Center on 9/11 and experienced a guiding presence who took his hand and led him out, or that of James Sevigny, a climber injured in an avalanche, who experienced a presence who gave him instructions and offered advice. By following the advice, Sevigny was able to walk to safety.

Scientific explanations for the phenomenon suggest biochemical reactions in the brain, or the brain misfiring under stress. But those explanations may not satisfy the people who have experienced a wise guide, leading them out of danger.

Section 5: Enhancing the vision

What is meant by 'enhancing the vision'?

This section returns to the vision of the ideal self created in Section 1 and provides activities that enrich and deepen the vision.

Why is it important to do this?

It is important to ensure that the vision, in order to have maximum motivational effect, is as vivid and elaborate as possible. If the steps in this chapter have been followed, the original vision will have been through various modifications and adjustments (substantiating, counterbalancing, aligning), and it is important to return to the vision itself at the end to ensure it is whole and not fragmented and that it is kept alive in the imagination.

What does 'enhancing the vision' entail?

It entails two distinct processes: (a) the enriching and elaboration of the original vision to make it more detailed, tangible and lasting; and (b) the provision of more precisely targeted, situation-specific visualisations aimed at getting the students to visualise their ideal L2 selves, coping successfully with situations relevant to their goals and learning circumstances (e.g. ordering meals in the L2, having a job interview in the L2, taking lecture notes in the L2). These two strands will be taken up and further developed throughout your course through activities in Chapter 3, 'Keeping the vision alive' chapter.

What, therefore, is the aim of this section?

The aim of this section is to create an enriched and motivating vision of the Ideal L2 Self.

How can this best be translated into practice in terms of usable classroom activities?

The activities in this section will be affective in nature, involving visualisation, simulations, photo-taking, poem and story creation, letter writing and board game design.

Does this involve any issues and problems?

See comments from the introduction to Section 1.

How can I best use these activities in my classroom to achieve the aim of this section?

The visualisations in Future Photo Album (Activity 30) are aimed at consolidating, adding to and enriching the vision, and could form an initial starting point. Thereafter, Future Self Portraits and Song of my Future Self (Activities 31 and 32) are aimed at adding more precise detail to the vision and at recording it for display in permanent form, while Fairytale (Activity 33) is aimed at getting the students to look back at their 'journey' so far and summarise it in written or graphic form.

Activity 30: Future Photo Album

Aim: To add more concrete and specific images to the concept of an ideal future self

Level: Elementary up

Time: 10–15 minutes

Materials: Small photo album with selection of photos, or music if preferred

Preparation: Rehearse the script

Language practice	
Functions	narrative, description
Skills	listening and speaking, writing in follow-up activity
Language areas	present simple, past simple, vocabulary for describing relationships and people

Procedure

1. Bring in a small photo album and use it to tell the students some things about your family, events in your life, etc. Tell students you are going to ask them to imagine their own albums – not with past photos but with photos from their future.

2. Ask students to close their eyes, and 'dictate' the visualisation.

3. When you have finished, ask them to open their eyes and discuss their imaginary future photo album with a partner.

4. This activity focuses on the general ideal future self. It can be targeted more precisely to the future L2 self with the alternative script below. It can be followed up by Activity 68 in the section on Developing Identity.

Script

Imagine . . . you are your future self . . . you have done many things in your life that you are proud of and many things that have made you happy . . . you are now going to open your photo album and look at some photos . . . you will see some people in your life whom you love and who have made you happy . . . you will see some places you have visited . . . and some events that have made you proud and happy . . .

Open your album at the first page . . . here is a picture of you . . . what do you look like? . . . where are you and what are you doing? . . .

Now turn over . . . here you are with some other people . . . who are they? . . . where are you all and what are you doing? . . . how are these people important to you in your life? . . . what do they give you? . . . and what do you give them? . . .

Now on the third page there are some pictures of important events in your life . . . an event that made you very happy . . . an event that was scary or difficult – but where you were successful . . . an event that made you proud . . .

Variation focusing on the L2 self

Imagine . . . you are your future self . . . you have done many things in your life that you are proud of and many things that have made you happy . . . you are now going to open your photo album and look at some photos . . . in this album you are going to see some photos of yourself as a successful (L2) . . . speaker . . . you will see some people you have talked to in (L2) . . . you will see some places you have visited, where you have talked in (L2) . . . and some situations where you have used (L2) . . .

Open your album at the first page . . . here is a picture of you . . . what do you look like? . . . where are you and what are you doing? . . .

Now turn over . . . here you are with some other people . . . who are they? . . . where are you all and what are you doing? . . . why are you speaking (L2) . . . ?

Now on the third page there are some pictures of some situations where you are using (L2) . . . successfully . . . there are three photos . . . where are you and what are you doing? . . . what are you saying or listening to? . . .

Activity 31: Future Self-Portraits

Aim: To create an image of the students' L2 selves situated in the L2 setting, in order to make the vision more concrete and tangible

Level: Elementary up

Time: 20–40 minutes, depending on the size of your class

Materials: Posters of scenes from the L2 country, or, if you have a screen and projector, photos of various settings, e.g. street scenes, outside a university, etc.; props such as tablecloth and coffee cups, menu, food items, desk and telephone to create settings such as café, shop or marketplace, office; choose these on the basis of what your students wrote in Activity 14; bring a camera to class

Preparation: Arrange the classroom so there is one area where posters can be put up or photo/slides displayed; in other areas create settings such as a café, office, market, etc.

Language practice	
Functions	description of places and actions
Skills	writing
Language areas	simple present, present continuous, there is/are

Procedure

1. The day before, explain what you are going to do: tell the students that you want to take photos of them in the situations they visualised in Activity 14 – at work talking on the phone in the L2, at university, chatting to a friend in a café, or as a traveller shopping or asking the way. Ask them to choose a situation and to wear or bring appropriate clothes to class (e.g. smart clothes for office, casual clothes, sunglasses, etc. for a tourist).

2. On the day, set up different areas of the classroom: one where you can display posters or project photos (e.g. of a street scene, market, students outside university, etc.), another with tables set up as café, a third with shop or market and a fourth with desk and telephone.

3. Ask students to go to the area they have chosen.

4. Take photos of them in the setting and doing the action they have chosen.

5. Get them to write a short description of the photo: where they are and what they are doing.

6. Make a classroom display of the photos.

Activity 32: Song of My Future Self

Aim:	To introduce the idea of a future L2 self and to get students to put in writing in a memorable form what their ideal L2 self would be
Level:	Pre-intermediate up
Time:	20–30 minutes
Materials:	None necessary
Preparation:	None

Language practice

Functions	description of places and actions
Skills	speaking, writing
Language areas	simple present, –ing, town places

Procedure

1. Write the following framework on the board, or give it out as a worksheet.

   My future self
   ____s at/in/on/along/round ____
   ____ing ____
   and ____ing ____

2. Students complete the poem-frame individually, for example:

   My future self
   Sits at a café
   Stirring my café au lait
   And talking French to a friend.

3. Group students in fours or fives and get them to put their verses together to make a complete poem, for example:

   My future self
   Sits at a pavement café
   Stirring my café au lait
   And talking French to a friend.

My future self
Stands at the street corner
Asking the way
And understanding the answer!

My future self
Wanders round the market
Sampling cheese and pâté
Drinking in the colours.

4. The finished poems can be displayed on posters.

Activity 33: Fairytale

Aim: To provide an imaginative representation of the journey towards the ideal self

Level: Intermediate up

Time: 30–40 minutes

Materials: Fairytale, fairytale lucky dip slips

Preparation: Find a fairytale from your culture, or the L2 culture. Copy enough fairytale lucky dip slips for everyone in your class to have five each. Cut them up and put them in five separate paper bags

Language practice

Functions	narrative, describing people and places
Skills	listening, speaking, writing
Language areas	past tenses, adjectives for people and places

Procedure

1. Brainstorm from the class what are some familiar elements of fairytales (e.g. giants, witches, wizards, heroes/heroines, princes/princesses, a journey, spells, tasks, transformations, a goal or grail, a wise counsellor, guide or good fairy, etc.).

2. Introduce to the class the idea that fairytales can tell us something about ourselves – the quest the hero or heroine follows is very often a journey to a future possible ideal self, involving various hardships and tasks, encounters with people, as well as objects or monsters that block the path and try to prevent the hero or heroine achieving the ideal. Very often there is also a guide or mentor figure who is on the hero/ heroine's side and offers wise advice. The elements of a fairytale can thus involve:

   - The Self: hero or heroine
   - The Ideal Self: the self the hero or heroine wishes to become
   - The Journey: the route he/she has to take to reach that goal

- Self Barriers: creatures that try to block the route and have to be overcome
- The Ought-to Self: a wise guide who can give advice.

3. Get students to classify elements they have identified during brainstorming under these headings: the Ideal Self (e.g. a prince instead of a frog, a princess instead of a servant), the Journey (e.g. hacking down the enchanted forest, climbing a mountain), Self Barriers (e.g. giants, trolls, dragons), the Ought-to Self (guide, cryptic counsellor, fairy godmother).

4. Get students to choose five slips from the lucky dip – one from each category – and to write a story based on those elements. You can help them by giving the structure on which quests and myths (and many Hollywood screenplays) are based:

   Initiating incident/call to action – meeting the mentor – the journey and trials (usually 3 trials) – approach to the inmost cave – the supreme ordeal – return with the elixir.

5. In pairs students tell stories and interpret them in terms of their own lives and goals.

Worksheet 1 Fairy tale lucky dip

Ideal selves slips	Journey slips	Self barriers slips	Ought-to selves slips	Task slips
Regaining human shape	Enchanted forest Mountain Deep lake	A giant who makes you his servant An old woman who invites you into her cottage where a magic bed makes you want to sleep forever A voice that sings so sweetly you want to listen to it forever	Wise woman	To find and bring back three golden apples
Transformation of status (e.g. servant to prince, beggar to princess)	Cave Waterfall Desert	A monster that bars the path A voice in a cave that tells you that you aren't brave enough A mirror that makes you want to look into it forever	Mysterious guide	To drink from a magic fountain; to do this you must first find three pieces of a map and put them together to find where the fountain is
Regaining power (e.g. magic power)	Tangled wood Dark river Quicksand	A winged horse that offers you a ride (but takes you in the wrong direction) A plant that winds itself around you and traps you A dragon that terrifies you	Wizard	To recover three jewels that are missing from a crown
Marriage to loved one	Rocks Moorland A sea voyage	A picture that invites you to step inside it and live in its magic land A group of villagers enjoying a feast who persuade you to stay A signpost that always points in the wrong direction	A fountain that talks	To find three keys which will unlock the doors in a tower where a magic potion is hidden

Photocopying of this worksheet is permitted: enlarge as necessary
© Jill Hadfield and Zoltán Dörnyei 2013

Chapter 2
Mapping the journey: from dream to reality

You must understand, I am not by nature a daydreamer. I try to control those parts of my life that can be controlled, to plan everything that I want to happen down to the most insignificant detail. I traffic in a world in which fractions of a second separate success and failure, so I'd visualized the 1996 Olympics down to the millisecond. I'd crafted a decade of dreams into ambitions, refined ambitions into goals, and finally hammered goals into plans.

(Michael Johnson, 1996: 14)

The component of the L2 Motivational Self System that this chapter focuses on – Mapping the Journey (or operationalising the vision) – implies activities of a very different kind from those in Chapter 1: Imaging identity. 'Operationalising' implies activities that are cognitive and practical in nature, rather than affective and imaginative. It implies activities that form a series of small steps in a logical progression, rather than the grander scale and more divergent nature of the activities in the first section. In order for a motivational programme to be effective and for the vision to be translated into reality rather than remain a fantasy, it is necessary to relate the imaginative to the practical, the affective to the cognitive and the creative to the logical.

At the same time, in order to appeal to different learning styles and retain the inspirational and enjoyable elements that imagination and affect impart to activities, we have also incorporated, alongside more logical and cognitive activities (such as discussion, classifying and ranking), activities such as letter writing, poster making, song writing which unite analysis and creativity.

There are four different sections in this chapter:

- From vision to goals
- From goals to plans

- From plans to strategies

- From strategies to achievement.

Each section is dynamic in nature, taking the students one step further along the route from vision to actuality. 'From vision to goals' takes students from the 'why' of motivation to the 'what': what exactly do I want to achieve; what are my goals? 'From goals to plans' takes students from the 'what' to the 'when': what tasks are involved in the goals I have specified for myself and when am I going to accomplish them? 'From plans to strategies' takes students from the 'when' to the 'how': how can I best accomplish the tasks I have set myself? Finally, 'From strategies to achievement' takes students from the 'how' to the 'who': who is going to witness and validate my achievement?

Each section has a predominant activity type depending on its aim. In Section 1 the main emphasis is on identifying goals. Predominant activity types therefore will involve listing, breaking down and classifying goals and objectives. Section 2 has planning and timetabling as its main aim. The activity types in this section will therefore involve ordering and prioritising. Section 3 involves introduction to a range of strategies and opportunities for the students to select those they find work best for them. This section consists of a range of activities following the sequence 'Identify – Try out – Discuss – Select'. Finally, Section 4, with its focus on making learning contracts and validating progress, contains activities following the sequence 'Contract – Evaluate – Validate – Reward'.

Section 1: From vision to goals

What is meant by translating 'vision' into 'goals'?

This is the first stage in the route from vision to reality. It entails revisiting the substantiated and enhanced vision arrived at through the activities in the previous chapter ('Imaging identity') and breaking this down into a list of long-term goals, then breaking these down further into short-term or weekly goals.

Why is it important to break the vision down into goals?

The vision of a future L2 self is too broad to form in itself a basis for action. It needs analysing into specific goals which are actionable. If it is not defined as a list of precise actionable goals, there is a danger that it will remain in the realms of dream and fantasy and never translate into reality.

What does defining goals entail?

It will entail in the first instance considering the initial vision, identifying the separate ambitions within it and using it as the basis for a list of long-term goals. It may then, depending on the constraints of the syllabus or course-book, involve a process of classifying the goals into those covered by the syllabus, those not covered but which could be added in, and those which will have to be met through self-study. The second half of the section involves a further process of breaking down the long-term goals into short-term or weekly goals, and breaking these down still further into a list of specific sub-goals.

What, therefore, is the aim of this section?

The aim of this section will be to provide activities that enable students to define long-term and weekly goals, which are:

(a) realistic and attainable,

(b) precisely specified,

(c) classified into those achievable through class and homework and those achievable through self-study.

How can this best be translated into practice in terms of usable classroom activities?

The process of identifying goals and ambitions essentially involves analysing and listing. Activity types which help students fulfil this aim are brainstorms, checklists, mindmaps and questionnaires. Examples of how to go about this process may be useful, and these have been provided in the form of a read-ing text with questions. The process also involves evaluation and discussion of the list of identified goals to ensure that they are achievable, comprehen-sive and realistic, and guided discussion activities are provided to help students achieve this. The process will also involve some alignment with the prescribed coursebook or existing syllabus to ensure that the goals are congruent with the course scope and sequence. Various classification and sorting activities will help students and teacher analyse which general aims can be met through whole class work and which more individual aims should be the focus of independent study. Finally, the goals determined by the class as a whole and individual students separately need to be made public and displayed as a reminder to give direction and purpose to the course. The poster-making activities in this section fulfil this purpose.

Does this involve any issues and problems?

One immediate problem is that students may find it hard to isolate and define a list of goals arising out of their initial vision, and equally hard to break these long-term goals into short-term ones. Students may also define goals that are unrealistic, unattainable or inadequate.

Another problem is any possible conflict or mismatch with a pre-existing syllabus. You and your class may find that your goals do not match the coursebook or syllabus you are following, or only match partially. Similarly, there may be a conflict of interest within the group: goals may not be shared or may be only partially shared among students.

Finally, there is the danger of losing sight of goals after the process of defining them is completed.

How can these issues best be dealt with?

The activities are structured so as to scaffold the students and help them through the process of identifying goals and breaking them down. There is also a concrete example given of the steps in the process of breaking vision down into goals.

The best way of ensuring that goals are realistic and attainable is to precede the activities in this section with those in 'Substantiating the vision' (Chapter 1, Section 2). It is in fact vital to ensure that the vision of the L2 self is grounded in reality before beginning the goal-defining process. The questionnaires and discussions in the section are also aimed at providing a further reality check.

The third problem really depends on how prescriptive your syllabus is. In extreme cases where there is a very rigid syllabus with no deviation possible, it would seem that any match of individual goals and externally prescribed syllabus may be difficult. In practice, however, rigid syllabuses are usually exam- or qualification-oriented, and passing the exam will probably be part of your students' vision of their future L2 selves; so, in such cases the actual mismatch will not be too great! In many cases, coursebook adaptation is possible. Activities 35 and 36 in Section 1 offer a framework for the traditional wisdom on using a coursebook: Supplement, Omit, Adapt and Replace, based on student aims. They also provide students with a framework for analysing which goals are shared, which are individual or idiosyncratic, and how far each of these can be met within the framework of the course; and alternatively, which goals could be the target of self-study.

These activities also raise awareness of the necessity of basing class work on group goals, and the importance of independent study for private goals.

Finally, the poster-making activities serve as a permanent reminder of the goals and a way of tracking progress.

How can I best use these activities in my classroom to achieve the aim of this section?

The activities in this section are in an order in which you could use them in the classroom, with more general activities such as defining long-term goals and considering examples coming before activities such as classifying goals, breaking goals down into short-term aims and making goal-reminders.

How much time you allocate to these activities depends very much on the constraints of your timetable and curriculum. However, goal setting is such an important part of motivation that it is worth allocating time to this through-out your course. It is important to establish the long-term goals and reach a class consensus, giving a sense of direction and purpose to the course from the very beginning, so it is worth allocating a lesson or two to the activities in the first half of Section 1 in the first week. Thereafter you could set aside a small amount of time at the beginning of each week for activities from the second half of the section to establish the week's short-term goals.

Your aims in selecting activities in the first week should be to choose activities that will appeal to your class with the following aims in mind:

- to enable students to list their long-term goals for the course
- to give students the opportunity to discuss and evaluate their goals
- to classify goals into those shared by the whole class that can be met through the syllabus, those shared by the whole class that can be added to the syllabus by you, and those which will have to be the focus of independent study
- to end up with a record of long-term goals in more permanent form.

The aim in subsequent weeks should be:

- to begin the week establishing a list of short-term goals for the week
- to classify these into classwork, homework and self-study goals.

Note: In Part III there is more advice on integrating activities into a course and adapting them to different levels and other contexts.

Activity 34: Wishlists

Aim: To translate the learners' substantiated visions into a list of long-term goals directly related to the course

Level: Intermediate up

Time: 40 minutes

Materials: Wishlist sheets and questionnaires

Preparation: Make one copy of the sentence frame sheet and questionnaire for each student

Language practice	
Functions	future wants, opinions
Skills	reading, writing, speaking
Language areas	want to, be able to, I think that . . .

Note: This activity follows on from the activities in the 'Substantiating the vision' section (Chapter 1, Section 2), for example 'Reality check 1 and 2', 'Leaf rating' or 'Vision revision'. It is important to have completed one of these with the students in order to have a written text as a basis for the current activity, but also, more importantly, to have completed a 'reality check' with the students so that their wishlist has some preliminary grounding in what is practicable and achievable.

Procedure

1. Make sure each student has a copy of his/her personal writing from an earlier activity from the 'Substantiating the vision' section.

2. Give each student a wishlist sheet.

3. Ask them to use the statements from their personal writing to complete the wishlist.

4. Put students in pairs to discuss their wishlists and give them a worksheet with discussion points.

5. Put pairs into fours to compare notes and make a summary.

6. Get a spokesperson from each group to give feedback from the summary to the class.

Worksheet 1 Wishlist

By the end of this course I want to be able to:

- _____
- _____
- _____
- _____
- _____
- _____
- _____
- _____

Worksheet 2

In pairs, compare your wishlists:

- What aims do you share?
- Are any aims unrealistic?
- Are any aims not useful?
- Are there any of your partner's aims that you haven't listed?
- Are these useful aims for you too?
- Do you want to add them to your list?

Use these questions to discuss your aims and to add or delete items from your list.

Activity 35: Syllabus Check

Aim:	To compare students' personal aims and align them with the demands of the syllabus/textbook in order to reach a class consensus on agreed class aims
Level:	Intermediate up
Time:	45 minutes
Materials:	Scope and sequence from syllabus or textbook; Worksheets 1 and 2; students' wishlists from Activity 34
Preparation:	Make one copy of the scope and sequence from your textbook or syllabus for each student, make one copy of Worksheet 1 for each student, and make a copy of Worksheet 2 for yourself.

Language practice	
Functions	future wants, opinions
Skills	reading, writing, speaking
Language areas	want to, be able to, I think that . . .

Note: Some of you may have the freedom to design your own syllabus and choose your own material for your courses, but it is often the case that you will be following a textbook or prescribed syllabus – with varying degrees of freedom. This activity is designed to help you choose among the options available to you for exploiting a syllabus or textbook (Supplement, Omit, Adapt, Replace) based on your students' needs and wants. It will also help increase student awareness of the necessity of having an agreed common core of aims and highlight for them which aims can be pursued in class together and which may have to be the subject of individual study.

Procedure

1. Make sure each student has a copy of the wishlist from Activity 34.

2. Give each student a copy of the syllabus/textbook scope and sequence and a copy of Worksheet 1.

3. Ask them to complete Worksheet 1, based on a comparison of the aims in their wishlist and the aims listed in the scope and sequence. You can get them to do this individually or, if you prefer, put them in the same groups of four from the previous activity.

4. Collect the completed tables.

5. Collate all the information using Worksheet 2.

6. Make a copy of your collated information for each student.

Worksheet 1 The syllabus and my ambitions

My personal aims that are covered in the syllabus	Personal aims that are not covered in the syllabus	Things in the syllabus that are not in my personal aims	
		Useful to me	Not so useful to me

Worksheet 2 Class aims, personal aims

Your aims that are covered in the coursebook	Aims that we can cover with extra material in class	Coursebook items we can leave out	Coursebook items that we need to keep (even if they aren't in your list of aims!)	Individual aims that you will need to work on by yourselves

Photocopying of this worksheet is permitted: enlarge as necessary
© Jill Hadfield and Zoltán Dörnyei 2013

Activity 36: Aims Poster

Aim: To reach a class consensus on agreed class aims and to display this as a statement in the form of a poster

Level: Intermediate up

Time: 45 minutes

Materials: Your completed Worksheet 2 from Activity 35 (Syllabus Check) plus large sheet of poster paper and strips of coloured paper

Preparation: Make one copy of your completed Worksheet 2 for each student; prepare a large sheet of poster paper by writing at the top:

Our Long-Term Goals

By the end of this course we will be able to . . .

Prepare a number of strips of coloured paper on which students can write the class goals.

Language practice	
Functions	future abilities, opinions
Skills	reading, writing, speaking
Language areas	want to, will be able to, I think that . . .

Procedure

1. Bring the copies of Worksheet 2, the poster and the paper strips to class. Give out a copy of Worksheet 2 to each student.

2. Explain to them that you have read carefully through all their Syllabus and Ambitions sheets and collected all the information on this Worksheet. The Worksheet shows what student aims are covered by the syllabus (Column 1). Explain to them that where a large number of students want something that is not on the syllabus/in the textbook, you will find some extra material to cover this (Column 2). Where the class feels a textbook item is not useful to them, it may be possible to omit this (Column 3), but, depending on either external requirements of the curriculum or your own

sense as a professional that the item in question is important, some items may have to be retained (Column 4). Finally, explain that in Column 5 you have collected 'minority aims': aims only expressed by a few students. Students may of course pursue these aims, but will have to devote individual self-study time to them.

3. Put students in pairs to read and discuss Worksheet 2, then group the pairs into fours and finally the fours into eights. Ask for any feedback from the groups of eight.

4. Put up the poster and give out an equal number of strips to each group. Explain that you will make a wall poster to list the long-term class goals. Later they can make a personal goal statement which will incorporate the class aims and their private aims. Allocate aims from Columns 1, 2 and 4 for students to copy onto the strips. When they have written them, they can come and paste them onto the poster.

Activity 37: Personal Goal Statements

Aim: To get students to write their own personalised goal state-ments, incorporating both agreed class goals and any extra individual goals they may have

Level: Intermediate up

Time: 20 minutes

Materials: Class goals poster from Activity 36 (Aims Poster), Worksheet 1 from Activity 35 (Syllabus Check), goal statement worksheet

Preparation: Make a copy of the goal statement worksheet. Fill in the class aims as stated on the poster. Then make a copy for each student.

Language practice	
Functions	future abilities, opinions
Skills	reading, writing,
Language areas	will be able to

Procedure

1. Give out copies of the goal statement sheet.

2. Explain to the students that this is their personalised list of goals and give them an opportunity to add their individual aims to the class goals.

3. Ask them to use the information they wrote down in Worksheet 1 to add their own individual goals and to decide how much self-study time a week they can devote to this.

4. When they have finished, they can sign it and get a partner to witness it.

Worksheet 1 My personal goal statement

These are our class goals

By the end of the course we will be able to

- _____
- _____
- _____
- _____
- _____

These are my additional personal goals

By the end of the course I will be able to

- _____
- _____
- _____
- _____

In order to do this I will

- _____
- _____
- _____
- _____

I will devote about . . . hours a week to self-study to achieve these goals.

Signed _____

Witnessed _____

Activity 38: From Reality Check to Goal Sheet: A Greek Example

Aim: To provide an example of how one student worked through the process of translating vision into personal long-term goal setting

Level: Intermediate up

Time: 20 minutes

Materials: Greek self reality check from Activity 9, the Greek textbook and my ambitions worksheet and My personal Greek goal statement

Preparation: Make one copy of each of the above for each student.

Language practice	
Functions	future wants, opinions
Skills	reading, speaking.
Language areas	want to, be able to, I think that . . .

Note: You can use this activity at any point in the above sequence if you want to provide a concrete example of how the process might work in practice.

Procedure

1. Give students a copy of the 'Greek self reality check' and the 'Greek textbook and my ambitions' worksheet.

2. Ask them to discuss in pairs, looking at the last two columns and suggesting reasons why the writer thinks these syllabus items are useful or not to her personally.

3. Collect ideas, then put the pairs into fours and ask them to discuss:

   • What personal goals does this student have that are not covered in the textbook?

   • What could she do about them – how could she achieve them?

   • How much time per week do you think she will need to spend in self-study?

Worksheet 1 The Greek textbook and my ambitions

My personal aims that are covered in the syllabus	Personal aims that are not covered in the syllabus	Things in the syllabus that are not in my personal aims	
		Useful to me	Not so useful to me
The textbook has: • Asking the way • Reading a menu • Ordering meals • Shopping • Food and drink • Greetings and introductions • Talking about family	• Reading street signs • Asking for change • Understanding instructions on parking meter • Renting a car I think I need to get more practice in reading fluently to be able to cope with things like street signs and instructions when in Greece. I probably need more listening practice than I can get in the class.	• In the Tourist Office • Likes and dislikes • Describing people • Sport and leisure • Describing towns	• Finding out about buses and trains • Describing rooms and houses

Worksheet 2 My personal Greek goal statement

These are our class goals. By the end of the course we will be able to:

- ask the way and understand directions
- read a menu and order meals in a restaurant
- go shopping
- greet and introduce ourselves
- talk about our families
- describe people
- talk about food and drink and say what we like and dislike
- talk about sports and leisure activities
- describe where we live
- describe our houses
- find out about transport
- ask for tourist information

These are my additional personal goals. By the end of the course I will be able to:

- rent a car
- understand street signs without having to stop the car to spell them out
- understand instructions on parking meters
- ask for change
- understand directions, etc. when people speak quickly

In order to do this I will:

- find some additional material on renting a car, using parking meters and asking for change
- put in some extra reading practice so I can read more quickly
- listen to the listening material from the course as often as possible in the car
- perhaps find another coursebook that covers the same topic areas in order to get more reading and listening practice.

I will devote about . . *2* . . hours a week self-study to achieve these goals.

Signed *Jill*

Witnessed **Charlie**

Activity 39: Base Camps

Aim: To identify in broad terms the week's learning goal

Level: Intermediate up

Time: 10 minutes

Materials: Large picture of a mountain, label, glue

Preparation: Find or draw a large poster of a mountain, prepare a strip of paper or label with the week's goal or goals stated in general terms.

Language practice	
Functions	stating aims and intentions
Skills	reading, listening
Language areas	be going to, will

Procedure

1. Bring a large poster of a mountain into class and pin it on the wall. Have prepared a label or strip of paper that you can stick onto the picture, stating the week's goal/topic in brief general terms (e.g. discussing relationships).

2. Stick the label on the poster at an appropriate point; for example, if this is the first week, stick it down at the base of the mountain.

3. Ask students in pairs to brainstorm what the week's topic might involve (e.g. listening to people discuss relationships, learning vocabulary for feelings, etc.).

4. Keep the poster on the wall. At the beginning of every week you can add a new label, progressively ascending the mountain. Have a flag ready for the top!

Activity 40: Goal Breakdown

Aim: To break down the week's goal into a series of sub-goals

Level: Intermediate up

Time: 20 minutes

Materials: Student brainstorms from Activity 39; week's list of aims and outcomes from relevant syllabus or textbook unit together with any additional aims and outcomes you have planned in; weekly personal goal statement

Preparation: Ask students to bring brainstorms with them, copy the unit aims together with your additional aims for each student, copy the weekly goal statement for each student

Language practice

Functions	future wants, opinions
Skills	reading, writing, speaking
Language areas	will be able to, want to, would like to, I think that . . .

Procedure

1. Put the pairs from the last activity together with another pair to make groups of four. Ask them to read each others' brainstorms from Activity 39 and compare them.

2. Give out the aims sheets you have prepared and ask them to discuss them, comparing them with their brainstorms.

3. Join each group of four into a group of eight to summarise to each other.

4. Ask each large group to give short feedback – anything extra they could add to the goals? Should these extra elements be class goals or personal goals? Have a brief class discussion to clarify this.

5. Give each student the weekly personal goal statement and get each student to make a week's goal statement, based on the discussion.

6. Collect these in.

Worksheet 1 My personal goal statement

These are our class goals for this week:

By the end of the week we will be able to

- --
- --
- --
- --
- --
- --

These are my additional personal goals for this week:

By the end of the week I will be able to

- --
- --
- --
- --
- --
- --

I will devote about . . . hours a week self-study to achieve these goals.

Signed _____

Activity 41: Goal Wheels

Aim:	To provide a collective statement of class and individual goals for the week
Level:	Intermediate up
Time:	15 minutes
Materials:	Student goal statements from Activity 40, goal wheel posters, segment strip of paper for each student
Preparation:	Prepare a goal wheel poster (see worksheet), read through student goal statements, write comments on them if necessary, prepare one strip of coloured paper for each student in the shape of the goal wheel segments

Language practice	
Functions	future wants, opinions
Skills	reading, writing, speaking
Language areas	will be able to, want to, would like to, I think that . . .

Procedure

1. Prepare a goal wheel poster and write the class aims in the central hub. Bring one 'segment' of coloured paper for each student, plus glue to class.

2. Give the students back their weekly goal statements and give each one a segment of coloured paper.

3. Put up the goal wheel. Explain that the hub is their collective aims. They are going to write their personal aims on the segments of coloured paper.

4. Students write their personal aims for the week on the paper segments and come up to glue them on the wheel.

5. Put the wheel up for classroom display.

Worksheet 1 Goal wheel

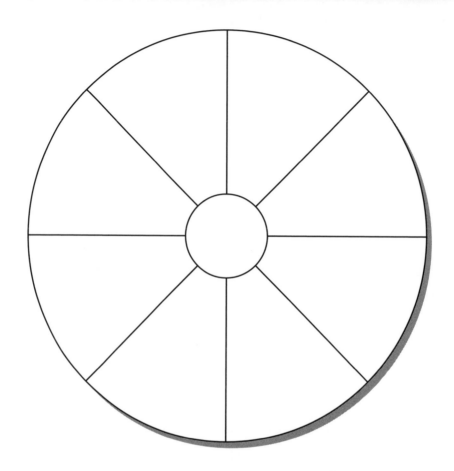

Section 2: From goals to plans

What is meant by translating 'goals' into 'plans'?

This is the process involved in making a study plan to realise the week's short-term goals.

Why is it important to translate goals into a study plan?

A goal is motivating as an ultimate destination, but in order to reach that destination you need a route map of exactly how you are going to get there, although of course the route may be negotiated as you and your learners move along it.

What does turning goals into plans entail?

It is a two-stage process. First (in the first half of Section 2) it involves the breaking down of short-term or weekly goals into a series of concrete tasks; so, for example, the goal of being able to order food in a restaurant will involve a series of sub-tasks such as learning food vocabulary, reading menus, listening to dialogues, practising requests, etc. The last activity in Section 2, then, entails the ordering and prioritising of the tasks into a weekly study plan.

What, therefore, is the aim of this section?

The aim of this section will be to provide activities that enable students to plan out their week's work with a timetable of tasks that are

- relevant and attainable
- precisely specified
- classified into those achievable through class and homework and those achievable through self-study.

How can this best be translated into practice in terms of usable classroom activities?

The process of identifying the series of tasks that form a roadmap to the goal essentially involves analysing and listing. Activity types in the first half of Section 2 are thus all variations on breaking down and listing, some of which ask students simply to list in a sequential way, some of which introduce a more visual and imaginative element.

The process also involves evaluation and discussion of the list of tasks to ensure that they are relevant to the goal, and guided discussion activities with teacher input are provided to help students achieve this and also to clarify which tasks will be completed in class or assigned for homework and which will be the focus of independent study. The process of turning a task list into a study plan involves ordering and prioritising, and the last activity in the second half of Section 2 will involve sequencing tasks into a timetable. For this task a number of variations are provided on the basic timetabling exercise, which introduce an imaginative and visual element.

Does this involve any issues and problems and how can these best be dealt with?

Students may find it hard to identify a list of tasks and to sequence these into a study plan. Therefore, the activities are structured so as to scaffold the students through teacher input, evaluation and discussion.

How can I best use these activities in my classroom to achieve the aim of this section?

It is up to you to select activities that you and your students will enjoy, but note that the task identification activities in the first half are a necessary prior step to the planning activities in the second half.

How much time you allocate to these activities depends very much on the constraints of your timetable and curriculum but it is worth spending a little time on Monday morning each week to identify tasks. If time is short, students could then write their study plan at home.

Note: In Part III there is more advice on integrating activities into a course and adapting them to different levels and other contexts.

Activity 42: Task List

Aim:	To break down the week's goals into a list of general tasks
Level:	Intermediate up
Time:	30 minutes
Materials:	Weekly goals statements or wheel poster from last section (Activities 40 and 41), task list worksheet
Preparation:	Make sure students have access to their goal statements or the wheel poster; make one copy of the task list worksheet and fill in the tasks that students will do in class and that will be set for homework in the coming week. Then make a copy for every student in your class

Language practice

Functions	intentions, obligations
Skills	reading, writing, speaking
Language areas	will, need to

Procedure

1. First copy the task list worksheet and fill in the parts you are responsible for setting (i.e. the classwork and the homework). In most cases you can probably take this directly from your textbook or syllabus unit, plus any supplementary materials you are adding. Make a copy for each student.

2. Give out the task list to students and ask them to look at their personal self-study goals for the week on their goal statements or wheel poster.

3. Ask them to identify broad areas for self-study to achieve their personal goals this week, for example some of these:
   - vocabulary learning
   - grammar study and practice
   - pronunciation practice
   - speaking practice
   - listening practice
   - reading
   - writing

4. Get them to fill these in on the task list.

Worksheet 1 Task list

This week in class we will:

For homework we will:

For self-study I will:

Activity 43: Taskmap

Aim:	To break down the week's general tasks into a list of precise tasks
Level:	Intermediate up
Time:	15 minutes
Materials:	Task list from last activity, examples of tasks sheet, pile of small pieces of paper for each student
Preparation:	Copy the example sheet if you want to use it, and prepare small pieces of paper for each student.

Language practice

Functions	intentions, obligations
Skills	reading, writing, speaking
Language areas	will

Procedure

1. Ask students to look at the very general tasks from the last activity. Put them in pairs and give each pair a pile of small pieces of paper. Ask them to think of more precise tasks in each category. They should write one task on each piece of paper. If you like you can give them the examples sheet at this point.

2. When they have finished, put the pairs into fours and give each four a large sheet of paper. Ask them to make a mindmap of the tasks they have come up with in the seven general areas.

3. Draw the beginnings of a mindmap on the board:

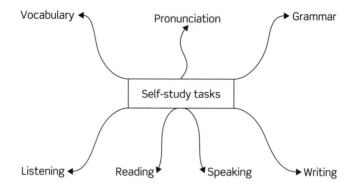

4. Ask one student from each group to come to the board and write their group's ideas under each category.

5. Ask students to choose particular tasks from those on the board to support the class and homework tasks or to focus on areas they find difficult and to write them in on their task list.

Worksheet 1 Examples of tasks

Vocabulary tasks	spend some time learning the week's vocabulary spend time learning extra vocabulary
Grammar tasks	study the grammar and make sure you understand it do extra exercises on the week's grammar
Pronunciation tasks	listen to the dialogues and do shadow reading or repetition focus on a particular pronunciation problem you have and find practice materials online or in the self-study centre
Speaking practice	practising dialogues from the coursebook practising with a friend
Listening practice	listening again to the material from the coursebook extra listening, e.g. films, songs, etc.
Reading tasks	reading authentic material, e.g. newspapers reading a graded reader
Writing tasks	rewriting homework assignments correctly extra writing practice, e.g. letters, stories, Facebook page

Note: The following activities are variations on the task list/mindmap with the same aim of breaking down goals into tasks. They have an additional purpose in that they invite students to form their own spatial 'map' of how the different tasks can relate to each other in a supportive or extensive role.

Activity 44: Mosaic

Aim: To break down the week's goals into a list of precise tasks

Level: Intermediate up

Time: 20 minutes

Materials: Weekly goals statements or goal wheel poster from Activities 40 and 41, Task List (Activity 42)

Preparation: Make sure students have access to their goal statements or the wheel poster; make one copy of the task list and fill in the tasks that students will do in class and that will be set for homework in the coming week; then make a copy for each student in your class.

Language practice

Functions	intentions, obligations
Skills	reading, writing, speaking
Language areas	will, need to

Procedure

1. Prepare an OHT poster or PowerPoint of the week's tasks that you will set in class or for homework and have this up at the front of the class.

2. Follow the mindmap procedure of the previous activity (Taskmap) to get students to identify precise tasks for self-study to support the class and homework tasks or to focus on areas they find difficult.

3. Get students to select tasks for their own self-study.

4. Give all students three sheets of paper in different colours. Get them to cut these into pieces and write one task on each piece, using the three different colours for class tasks, homework and self-study. They can glue these to make a mosaic showing how the different tasks fit together to lead on from and reinforce each other.

Variations

These variations fulfil the same purpose but are designed to provide variety.

Jigsaw

Follow Steps 1–3 above but replace Step 4 as below:

- Give each student the three different coloured jigsaw outlines. Get them to cut these into pieces and write one task on each piece, using the three different colours for class tasks, homework and self-study. They can put these together to make a jigsaw showing how the different tasks fit together to lead on from and reinforce each other.

Task tree

Follow Steps 1–3 above, but replace Step 4 as shown below:

- Give each student a 'task tree' (Worksheet 2). Get them to write the class tasks on the trunk and the homework on the branches. Get students to select tasks for their own self-study and to draw them on the task tree in the form of leaves.

Worksheet 1 Jigsaw outline

Photocopying of this worksheet is permitted: enlarge as necessary
© *Jill Hadfield and Zoltán Dörnyei 2013*

Worksheet 2 Task tree

Activity 45: Slicing Up the Cake

Aim:	To break down the week's goals into a list of precise tasks and allocate timing
Level:	Intermediate up
Time:	15 minutes
Materials:	Weekly goals statements (from Activity 40), Task List (Activity 42), cake picture worksheet
Preparation:	Make sure students have access to their goal statements; make one copy of the task list and fill in the tasks that students will do in class and that will be set for homework in the coming week; then make an OHT to show the class

Language practice	
Functions	intentions, obligations
Skills	reading, writing, speaking
Language areas	will, need to

Procedure

1. Prepare an OHT poster or PowerPoint of the week's tasks that you will set in class or for homework and have this up at the front of the class.

2. Get students to brainstorm additional tasks for self-study in pairs or small groups to support the class and homework tasks or to focus on areas they find difficult. Collect suggestions from the groups and write them on the board or an OHT.

3. Get students to select tasks for their own self-study.

4. Give each student a 'cake picture'. Get them to divide it into three 'slices' of different sizes showing relative proportions of time to be spent on class tasks, homework and self-study and to write the tasks in each slice.

Worksheet 1 Cake

Activity 46: Study Plan

Aim:	To organise the week's goals into a timetable
Level:	Intermediate up
Time:	15 minutes
Materials:	Student-created posters from Activities 43, 44 or 45; blank timetable
Preparation:	Make a copy of the timetable and fill in the class and home-work goals for each day; make a copy for each student.

Language practice	
Functions	intentions, obligations
Skills	reading, writing, speaking
Language areas	will, need to

Procedure

1. Give each student a copy of the timetable.

2. Ask them to look at whichever of the activities you have done previously to define their self-study tasks (Activities 43, 44 or 45). Get them to fill these in on the timetable, indicating which days/evenings they will work and how long they will spend.

3. Get students to compare timetables in pairs and give each other feedback.

Variations

Note: The following activities are variations on the timetable and have the same aim of sequencing tasks into plans. They will appeal to more visual or more imaginative students and can be used as an alternative to the time-table to provide variety.

Intention bubbles

1. Give each student a copy of the poster.

2. Ask them to look at whichever of the activities you have done previously to define their self-study tasks. Get them to fill these in the thought bubbles, one for each day.

3. Get students to compare intention bubbles in pairs and give each other feedback.

Building bricks

1. Give each student a copy of the tower.

2. Ask them to look at whichever of the activities you have done previously to define their self-study tasks. Get them to fill these in on the floors (i.e. days) of the tower, indicating which days/evenings they will work (obviously they don't need to work every day!) and how long they will spend.

3. Get students to compare towers in pairs and give each other feedback.

Roadmap

1. Make a copy of the roadmap and fill in the class and homework goals for each 'bend in the road'. Each bend represents a day and has three sections, one for classwork, one for homework and one for self-study. Make a copy for each student.

2. Give each student a copy of the roadmap.

3. Ask them to look at whichever of the activities you have done previously to define their self-study tasks. Get them to fill these in on the bends (i.e. days) of the road, indicating which days/evenings they will work (obviously they don't need to work every day!) and how long they will spend.

4. Get students to compare maps in pairs and give each other feedback.

Worksheet 1 Study plan

	Mon	Tues	Wed	Thurs	Fri	Sat	Sun
Classwork							
Homework							
Self-study							

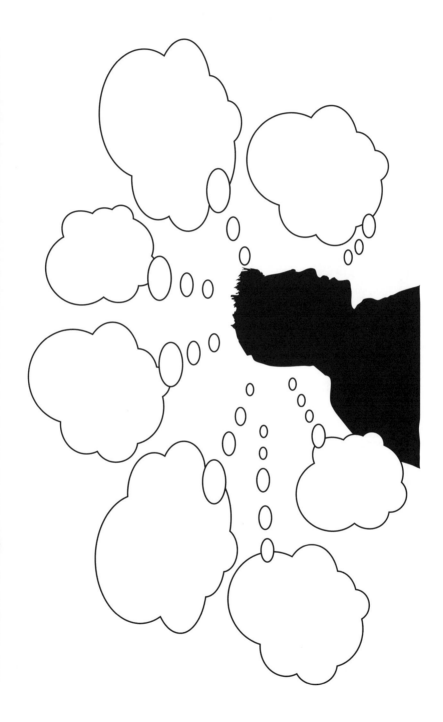

Worksheet 3 Tower Block

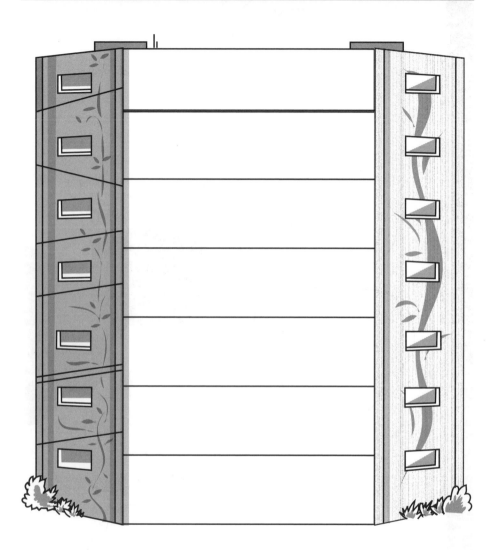

Worksheet 4 Roadmap

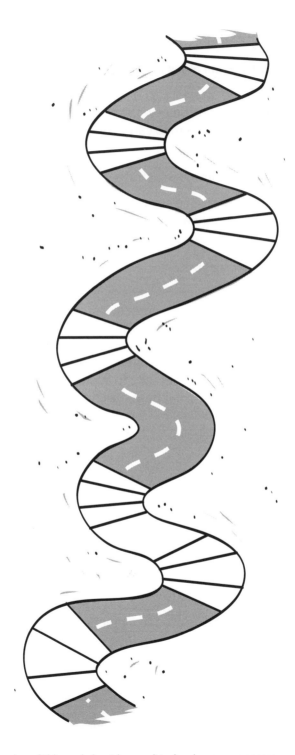

Photocopying of this worksheet is permitted: enlarge as necessary

Section 3: From plans to strategies

What is meant by 'From plans to strategies'?

It means introducing students to a range of helpful techniques to improve their study efficiency, and helping them to select those which work best for them, in order to enable them to carry out their study plans more effectively.

Why is it important to introduce strategies?

Students may not have good study habits, or may be unaware of techniques they could use to help them study.

What does introducing strategies entail?

It will entail raising students' awareness of the ways in which they work and their preferred working styles, introducing and trying out some techniques that might help them to work more productively, getting them to discuss and evaluate these and finally selecting those that work best for them. The first half of Section 3 contains 'achievement strategies': study techniques that can be used across a range of tasks to improve learning, for example by aiding memorisation or improving note-making techniques. The second half of Section 3 contains 'avoidance strategies': techniques that can be used to overcome barriers to learning, for example by avoiding distraction or managing time better.

What, therefore, is the aim of this section?

The aim of this section will be to introduce students to a range of strategies both to improve learning techniques and to overcome self barriers to learning, to give them opportunities for discussion and evaluation of these strategies and to get them to select those that work best for them.

How can this best be translated into practice in terms of usable classroom activities?

The process described above will involve the following basic steps:

- identifying work style and preferred strategies
- introduction to and trial of new strategies

- discussion and evaluation
- summarising and selection.

These steps define four activity prototypes:

- identify and discuss
- read about and discuss
- try out and discuss
- select and justify.

Within these prototype activities, a wide variation is possible: 'identify and discuss' may involve brainstorms, questionnaires, ranking, drawing, surveys, and making songs and jingles. 'Read and discuss' can involve jigsaw reading and roleplay as well as reading comprehension. 'Try out and discuss' involves trial of a range of techniques such as relaxation or using imaginative association. Finally, 'select and justify' involves making adverts, raps and advice letters.

Does this involve any issues and problems?

Students may be unsure of which approach will work best for them, or they may have habits that they have fallen into and which are difficult to change.

The timing and organisation of a strategies programme presents something of a dilemma. If strategies are introduced all at once at the beginning of the course, students may get confused; if they are introduced gradually in, say, 15 minute per week slots, students may not discover a strategy that works really well for them until late in the course.

How can these issues best be dealt with?

The discussion and evaluation activities are designed to get students to think critically and judge what strategies will work best for them. Existing study habits are only a problem if they are unproductive, in which case students may welcome alternative ideas and suggestions. It is important to avoid pre-scription – what works well for one student may not work for another.

The timing of the awareness-raising activities presents more of a problem. Possibly the best solution is to combine the two approaches: to begin with a short general overview or 'strategies fair', followed by a more gradual drip-feed approach as the course unfolds.

How can I best use these activities in my classroom to achieve the aim of this section?

It does not matter in which order you use the activities in this section, though if you intend to use the more general questionnaires at the beginning of Section 3 you should programme them in before the more detailed work on particular strategies.

How much time you allocate to these activities depends very much on the constraints of your timetable and curriculum. However, study strategies are such an important part of effective study that it is worth allocating time to this throughout your course – see suggestions in Part III.

Your aims in selecting activities should be to choose activities that will appeal to your class and that they will find useful, with the following aims in mind:

- to acquaint students with a range of strategies both for improving study skills and for overcoming barriers to learning

- to give students the opportunity to try out, discuss and evaluate which strategies work well for them.

Note: In Part III there is more advice on integrating activities into a course and adapting them to different levels and other contexts.

Activity 47: Work Style

Aim:	To initiate a discussion on students' different study habits and working styles
Level:	Intermediate up
Time:	40 minutes
Materials:	Discussion sheet worksheet
Preparation:	Make one copy of the discussion sheet for each student.

Language practice	
Functions	discussing habits, preferences and routines
Skills	reading, writing, speaking
Language areas	like -ing, present simple + frequency adverbs

Procedure

1. Make copies of the discussion sheet and give one to each student.

2. Ask them to work individually to answer the questions.

3. Put them in pairs to discuss their answers.

4. Put the pairs in fours to compare answers. Get them to make a 'report sheet' showing the way their group answered the discussion questions. This can be in the form of a verbal report (e.g. *Three of us prefer to work alone, but one prefers to work with a friend*) or in the form of a mindmap or pie chart showing the preferences of the group.

5. Take a class survey on study habits based on the answers to the questions. You can do this by asking for oral summaries or by collecting in the 'reports' and collating them.

6. Use the survey to initiate a discussion. Do students feel they work best in this way? Is there anything they would like to change?

Worksheet 1 Discussion sheet: you and the way you study

1. *How* do you like to study?

   - alone or with others
   - with no distractions or with background noise (e.g. music)
   - by reading or by listening
   - moving around or using your hands when you study
   - writing notes to summarise information or making tables and diagrams.

2. *What kind of* study aids do you use?

   - lists
   - labels
   - a notebook
   - cards
   - computer or mobile phone
   - others.

3. *When* do you work?

   - morning/afternoon/evening
   - at a set time every day
   - randomly
   - at spare moments, e.g. waiting for the bus.

4. *What* do you study?

   - going over class work or reading/listening to new material
   - from books
   - from newspapers and magazines
   - from TV and radio
   - from the Internet.

5. When you study, do you spend a long time focusing on a short text/vocabulary list/grammar rule or do you read and listen to longer texts without working in detail on the language?

Activity 48: Study Habits

Aim:	To initiate a discussion on students' different study habits and working styles
Level:	Intermediate up
Time:	40 minutes
Materials:	Questionnaire
Preparation:	Make one copy of the study habit questionnaire for each student.

Language practice	
Functions	discussing habits, preferences and routines
Skills	reading, writing, speaking
Language areas	like -ing, present simple + frequency adverbs

Procedure

1. Give each student a copy of the study habit questionnaire.

2. Put them in pairs and get them to ask each other the questions.

3. Group the pairs into large groups (6–8) and get them to make a pie chart of the answers showing the percentage of people in each group who have used the activities mentioned.

4. Get the group to discuss which activities they would like to try out and to write a summarising paragraph beneath the pie chart under the heading: 'Study ideas we would like to try out'.

Worksheet 1 Study habit questionnaire

When you study by yourself, do you do any of the following?

1. Write sentences to practise vocabulary or grammar that have a personal meaning for you.

2. Use association to remember vocabulary (e.g. linking a new word with a mental image, picture or memory).

3. Make notes.

4. Make vocabulary or grammar cards.

5. Make labels or posters with new words or grammar structures to stick around the house.

6. Keep a vocab or grammar notebook.

7. Use computers or mobile phones to help you remember vocabulary.

8. Work with a friend to test each other or play a game.

9. Set aside a specific time everyday for work.

10. Use 'dead time' (e.g. time waiting at bus stop, time driving to work).

11. Use external resources (e.g. read newspapers, listen to radio and TV, watch films, Internet).

12. When studying, work intensively (i.e. concentrating on learning a grammar point or new words, or reading a short text in detail) or extensively (e.g. reading a graded reader, watching a film).

Activity 49: Time Management

Aim: To introduce students to some ideas for using time productively

Level: Intermediate up

Time: 15 minutes

Materials: None

Preparation: None

Language practice	
Functions	talking about preferences, giving opinions, making suggestions
Skills	speaking, writing
Language areas	I'd like to . . . , we could, shall we . . . , I think that . . .

Procedure

1. Brainstorm with students a list of 'dead time': time when you are doing something boring that does not involve mental activity (e.g. waiting for the bus, driving to work, doing the ironing).

2. Ask them to calculate approximately how much time they spend doing these activities per day.

3. Ask them to calculate how much time they spend in class, how much time they spend on homework and how much time they are prepared to spend on independent study.

4. Get them to make a pie chart showing the relative proportions of class work, homework, independent study and dead time.

5. Brainstorm a list of activities that they could do in the dead time (e.g. listening to a CD in the car, revising vocabulary at the bus stop, etc.).

Activity 50: Try This!

Aim: To get students to summarise their preferred self-study strategies

Level: Intermediate up

Time: 20 minutes

Materials: Poster paper and coloured pens for each group of three or four

Preparation: None

Language practice	
Functions	giving advice, persuading
Skills	writing, speaking, reading
Language areas	imperatives, should, will

Procedure

1. Put students in small groups and ask them to brainstorm strategies that they have found particularly useful in their own learning experience in the past. Ask them to make a list of all the effective strategies mentioned.

2. Give each group some coloured pens and a big sheet of paper. Ask them to choose three favourite strategies from their list and write an advert for these, saying how they use them and why they are useful. The goal is to persuade other students to try them!

3. Pin the adverts round the room.

4. You may conclude with a class vote on which advert was the most persuasive (students are not allowed to vote for the adverts that their own group produced).

Activity 51: Great Expectations

Aim: To focus on and clarify expectations of self-study outcomes and to introduce the notion of rewarding yourself for fulfilling expectations

Level: Intermediate up

Time: 45 minutes

Materials: Expectations worksheet

Preparation: Ask students to come to class with a precise self-study task; make copies of the worksheet for each student

Language practice	
Functions	stating outcomes and intentions
Skills	depending on self-study area chosen
Language areas	will have, in order to, will

Procedure

1. The day before, explain that the next class will be 'guided self-study', where they will do an exercise aimed at helping them to focus on their aims, define what they expect to be able to do and evaluate how well it went. Ask students to come to class with a precise self-study task, to take about 20 minutes (e.g. a list of words to learn, a grammar point they need to practise, a reader to read, a piece of writing to do or – if you have individualised listening facilities such as a language lab, computer lab or a self-access centre – some listening or pronunciation practice).

2. Make a copy of the 'expectations' sheet for each student and give these out at the start of the class. Get students to fill these out individually, then put them in pairs to read each other's and comment, according to the following criteria:

   • Are the expectations too high?
   • Are they too low?
   • Are the steps appropriate and helpful?
   • Can you make any suggestions to help your partner achieve his/her aim?

3. Give a period of time – about 20 minutes – over to self-study. Then ask them to fill in the 'outcome' and 'reason'.

4. At the end, put the students in pairs with their original partners to discuss whether they achieved their aims and comment on their learning experience.

5. Bring the pair discussion back to the whole class, collecting feedback and summarising it. The aim is that they have an outline procedure to follow every time they sit down to start independent study, with a clear idea of pitfalls to avoid, such as imprecise expectations, unhelpful steps, etc. Depending on your class, you may need to repeat this activity a few times.

6. Finally, ask students to complete the 'rewards' section, stating what they will do tonight and the rewards they will give themselves. Suggest some examples: listening to a song, playing a (short) computer game, having a coffee . . . The next day collect feedback on how this worked.

Worksheet 1 Expectations

Task

I have 20 minutes to study. By the end of that time I will have _____

_____

Steps

In order to do this I will [complete as many steps as you need]:

1. _____

2. _____

3. _____

4. _____

5. _____

6. **My partner's suggestions** _____

Outcome

I achieved this (please encircle your answer):

Very well   Well   Quite well   Not very well

Reason

This was because _____

My partner's comments _____

_____

Learning from experience

Next time I will _____

_____

Reward!

Tonight I will spend _____ minutes doing _____

At the end I will have _____

My reward for doing this is _____

Activity 52: Distraction Reduction

Aim:	To identify recurrent personal distractions and to identify steps to take to eliminate these or use them as rewards
Level:	Intermediate up
Time:	25 minutes
Materials:	Distraction jingles sheet
Preparation:	Make one copy of each jingles sheet for each group of three or four students; make one copy of distraction contract for each student

Language practice

Functions	making excuses, habits, intentions
Skills	writing, speaking, reading
Language areas	I'll (just) . . . , shall, present perfect, present simple, can, going to

Procedure

1. Introduce the idea of distractions: tell the students a few ways you distract yourself from getting down to work and ask for suggestions from the class about ways they put off working or get distracted. List some of these on the board.

2. Give out the distraction jingles sheet and read the first verse with the students.

3. Divide the students into four groups and get each group to complete a verse. Alternatively get each group to complete the whole jingle, using distraction ideas from all the members.

4. Read the whole jingle at the end with each group reading their own verse/jingle. You can make a poster for class display.

5. Then put students in pairs and ask them to identify the distractions they enjoy the most (e.g. cleaning the fridge and texting a friend may both be distractions, but you may enjoy one more than the other!).

6. Introduce the idea that distractions can become rewards: students can still do the activities that distract them, but as a reward for work done rather than a way of avoiding starting work.

7. Give out the distraction contract sheets.

8. Get students to complete this individually, then ask for ideas for the contracts and rewards. Have a discussion on what is realistic. One key is stipulating a reasonable amount of time for work and also for distractions (feedback from teenagers suggests 40–45 minutes for work then 10–15 minutes' distraction). Another key is varying indoor distractions (e.g. listening to iPod) with outdoor activity and exercise. Students can then amend their contracts if necessary.

9. Finally, put them in pairs to share their contracts and witness each other's.

10. Ask them to try to carry it out that evening and get feedback the next day.

Worksheet 1 Distraction jingles

I'll just check my cellphone
I'll just look and see
I'll listen to my iPod
And then I'll watch TV

I'll just _____

I'll just have some tea

I'll just _____

Has anyone emailed me?

I'll just _____

I'll just send a text

I'll just _____

And clean the fridge out next.

I'll just _____

I'll just go on Facebook

I'll just _____

I've nothing left to cook.

I'll just _____

I'll just wash my hair

I'll just _____

And now what shall I wear?

Worksheet 2 Distraction contracts

The main ways I distract myself are:

- _____
- _____
- _____
- _____

The distractions I most enjoy are:

- _____
- _____
- _____

From now on I am going to use these distractions as rewards:

After _____ minutes' work I can _____ for _____ minutes

After _____ minutes' work I can _____ for _____ minutes

After _____ minutes' work I can _____ for _____ minutes

After _____ minutes' work I can _____ for _____ minutes

Signed _____

Witnessed _____

Activity 53: Allocating Time

Aim:	To identify good ways of allocating and managing time to ensure variety and reduce boredom
Level:	Intermediate up
Time:	25 minutes
Materials:	Timetable task
Preparation:	Make one copy of the timetable for each pair of students

Language practice	
Functions	making suggestions, stating opinions, hypothesis
Skills	writing, reading, speaking
Language areas	let's, shall we, what about, I think that . . . , should, if . . . would, could

Procedure

1. Introduce the idea of boredom control: tell the students a few ways you try to manage your time so that you don't get bored or burnt out (e.g. by varying tasks, by doing the things you hate in small doses interspersed with tasks you enjoy, by working in manageable chunks of time, etc.) and ask for suggestions from the class. List some of these on the board.

2. Put students in pairs and give out the timetable task sheet.

3. Get students to decide how they would work out their homework time-table, based on the principles at the top of the page.

4. When they have finished, put the pairs in fours to compare timetables.

5. Ask for feedback on ideas from each group.

Worksheet 1 Timetable task

Next week, you have the following things to do:

- a class presentation with a partner on Monday morning
- a vocab test on Tuesday
- a grammar test on Wednesday
- finishing reading a graded reader for a group discussion on Thursday (you have 20 pages left)
- handing in a 500-word (2-page) essay on Friday.

It's Saturday. Work out how you are going to do the following things:

- rehearse the presentation
- revise for the vocabulary test
- revise for the grammar test
- finish the reader
- write the essay: brainstorm, outline, first draft, final draft.

You normally spend a couple of hours on homework and study. You get home about 4 p.m. after class finishes. You want to go out with friends about three times this week.

Plan a study timetable, taking the following things into account:

- You concentrate best for about 40–45 minutes. It's a good idea to have a short break and change the activity after that.
- You need to prioritise so more urgent tasks come before other less urgent tasks.
- Varying tasks prevents boredom.

Can you break tasks down into short 40–45 minute blocks?

Can you prioritise your tasks so that the most urgent ones come first?

Which tasks do you enjoy? Which ones do you dislike? Can you alternate them – or use the enjoyable tasks as rewards?

Rewards are motivating – how can you reward yourself for work done?

Time	Sat	Sun	Mon	Tues	Wed	Thurs	Fri

Activity 54: Light Fantastic

Aim: To explore (legitimate) ways of using fantasy and humour as boredom control strategies

Level: Intermediate up

Time: 45 minutes

Materials: Vocabulary, grammar and writing task worksheet

Preparation: Copy the task worksheet for each student or substitute your own tasks to suit the level you are teaching

Language practice

Functions	depending on tasks selected
Skills	depending on self-study area chosen
Language areas	depending on tasks selected

Procedure

1. Use the three tasks provided or substitute more appropriate ones for your students. Copy the task sheet for each student. Divide students into three groups and assign each group one task.

2. Ask them to work together to complete the task.

3. Regroup the students into groups of three so that each new group contains at least one member of the three original groups.

4. Ask the groups of three to share the ideas they had for enlivening the materials using humour or fantasy.

5. Ask for feedback from the groups.

Worksheet 1 Task sheet: three boring tasks

1. **Vocabulary task:** Use the following words in sentences: seaside, planet, umbrella, envelope, canoe, waving.

2. **Grammar task:** Write five sentences using the past simple.

3. **Writing task:** Write a thank you letter.

Discuss how you could use fantasy and humour to make the tasks more interesting. For example:

- In the vocabulary task, you could make all the sentences connect to make a story about, for example, an alien from another planet who arrived in a canoe . . . ☺

- In the grammar task you could write improbable sentences from your diary last week: *Monday: I met Lily Allen at a party . . .*

- In the writing task you could write a thank you letter to someone unlikely:

  Dear Puss,

  Thank you for sitting next to me and purring so loudly yesterday. It really cheered me up . . .

Activity 55: Chill

Aim:	To introduce students to some relaxation techniques
Level:	Intermediate up
Time:	25 minutes
Materials:	Calm music, visualisation script, relaxation script, meditation script
Preparation:	Find a CD of very calm music, familiarise yourself with the three scripts.

Language practice

Functions	stating outcomes and intentions
Skills	depending on self-study area chosen
Language areas	will have, in order to, will

Procedure

1. Explain to students you are going to introduce them to four very simple five-minute relaxation techniques that they can use to clear their minds, get rid of stress and prepare for study.

2. Technique 1: *Listen to calming music.* Ask students to close their eyes and relax. Tell them you are going to play some music and they can just let anything – or nothing – come into their minds as they listen. Play the CD for about five minutes.

3. Technique 2: *Imagine a nice place.* Ask students to close their eyes and imagine as you dictate a visualisation script.

4. Technique 3: *Empty your mind.* Ask students to sit comfortably and close their eyes. Dictate the meditation script.

5. Technique 4: *Relax completely.* Ask students to sit comfortably or to lie on the floor if possible. Dictate the relaxation script.

6. Put students into groups or pairs and get them to discuss which technique worked best for them – which could they imagine using in future to prepare themselves for studying and relieve stress? Are there any other techniques they use?

7. Get feedback from the class.

Visualisation script

Imagine you are in your favourite place. It is a place that means a lot to you and where you feel comfortable and relaxed. It could be a place that is cosy and secure . . . like sitting by the fireside at home, curled up in a comfy chair . . . it could be a place that is quiet and calm . . . like being in a clearing in the centre of a forest with tall trees overhead and sunlight through the leaves . . . perhaps you can hear birdsong and hear the splashing of a stream . . . it could be a place that inspires you . . . like being on top of a mountain on a clear day with a beautiful view in front of you . . . or on a white sand beach with blue waves crashing on the shore . . . choose a place and imagine you are there . . . How do you feel?

Meditation script

Sit on the floor and find a comfortable position . . . start to relax . . . start from your head . . . let it feel heavy . . . very heavy . . . and let it drop . . . when your head feels heavy, continue down to your shoulders . . . drop your shoulders and relax . . . as you start to relax breathe deeply in and out . . . let your body and your legs sink into the ground . . . now you are totally relaxed . . . continue relaxing . . . feeling as if your body is sinking into the ground . . . now begin to focus on your breathing . . . breathe in and out . . . in and out . . . concentrate on your breathing . . . empty your mind . . . just focus on your breathing . . . in and out . . . think about nothing but your breathing . . . in . . . and out . . . when you think about something else come back to breathing . . . you feel peaceful and calm . . .

Relaxation script

Close your eyes . . . find a comfortable position . . . breathe deeply . . . take long breaths in . . . and out . . . try to direct your thoughts to what is happening here and now . . . in the room around you . . . be aware of sounds in the room around you . . . now be aware of how you are sitting . . . begin to relax . . . begin by relaxing your toes . . . your feet . . . they feel heavy now . . . now your legs . . . let them feel relaxed . . . now your body and your shoulders . . . drop your shoulders . . . your arms . . . your hands . . . now your neck . . . your head . . . your whole body is relaxed . . .

Activity 56: Positive Thinking

Aim: To focus on the importance of positive thinking

Level: Intermediate up

Time: 45 minutes

Materials: Quotations worksheet, film clip

Preparation: Make a copy of the quotations worksheet for each student

Language practice	
Functions	stating outcomes and intentions
Skills	depending on self-study area chosen
Language areas	will have, in order to, will

Procedure

1. If possible, as an introduction, play the students a clip from a film where an unconfident character is encouraged to think more positively about him/herself (e.g. Angie encouraging Oscar in *Shark tale*, the nuns in *The sound of music* encouraging Maria to 'Climb every mountain', the song 'I have confidence in confidence itself', etc.). Ask them what the message of the extract is, trying to elicit the ideas of self-belief, positive thinking and attitude as enabling forces.

2. Give out the quotations sheet and ask students to discuss it in pairs.

3. Put pairs into fours to share ideas and give them one further question. In what ways could one of these quotations help you with your study?

4. Ask for feedback from the groups.

5. Then put the fours into eights and ask a further question. Can you come up with a list of ways in which you could put yourself in a positive mood for study? When would it be useful to do these things (e.g. at the beginning of the day, before sitting down to self-study, before exams, etc.)?

Worksheet 1 Quotations: positively charged

Here are some things that famous people have said about positive thinking. Please decide:

- Which quotations ring true for you?
- Are there any that you don't think are right?
- Can you relate any to your own experience?
- If you had to choose one as a motto, which one would you choose?

Perseverance is not a long race. It is many short races one after another. (Walter Elliott, Catholic priest and writer)

Having a positive mental attitude is asking how something can be done rather than saying it can't be done. (Bo Bennett, businessman and writer)

Wherever a negative thought concerning your personal power comes to mind, deliberately voice a positive thought to cancel it out. (Norman Vincent Peale, author of *The power of positive thinking*)

Once you replace negative thoughts with positive ones you'll start having positive results. (Willie Nelson, country and western singer)

A pessimist sees the difficulty in every opportunity, an optimist sees the opportunity in every difficulty. (Winston Churchill, statesman)

Positive anything is better than negative nothing. (Elbert Hubbard, editor and writer)

The basis of optimism is sheer terror. (Oscar Wilde, playwright)

I let negativity roll off me like water off a duck's back. If it's not positive, I didn't hear it. If you can overcome that, fights are easy. (George Foreman, boxer)

Activity 57: Favourite Workplace

Aim:	To get students to identify factors contributing to a good work environment and to identify steps they could take to create this for themselves
Level:	Intermediate up
Time:	25 minutes
Materials:	Some pictures of workplaces, poster in circular shape, slips of coloured paper, favourite workplaces worksheet, ratings sheet
Preparation:	Find some pictures of tables/desks/offices, ranging from cluttered and noisy to calm and well-ordered, to show to the class; copy one favourite workplace worksheet and one ratings worksheet for each student

Language practice	
Functions	stating preferences, making comparisons, giving reasons
Skills	speaking, writing, reading
Language areas	like, prefer, comparatives and superlatives, because

Procedure

1. If possible, find some pictures to show the class of tables/desks/offices ranging from cluttered and noisy to calm and well-ordered. Elicit some reactions from the students. Where would be easiest to work? Where would be most difficult? Why?

2. Put students into groups of three or four and give out the favourite workplace worksheets, one to each student.

3. Ask students to use the scenarios in the worksheet as a basis for discussion of where they could work well and where they could not work.

4. Ask for feedback from the groups.

5. Give out the ratings worksheet to each student and get groups to add places where they have worked.

6. Get them to rate the workplaces according to distraction and relaxation and to compare their ratings within their groups.

7. Get them to discuss what activities might work best in different places and how they could possibly vary workplace to reduce boredom and stimulate interest in work.

8. Now ask students each to draw a plan of their ideal workplace.

9. Put them in small groups to compare their plans and discuss the factors that make it ideal for them.

10. Get each group to compile a list of factors contributing to a good work environment. Get feedback from the groups and summarise everyone's ideas in a general list on the circular poster. Put the poster up where everyone can see it.

11. Ask students to think about their own work environment at home. How is it different from the ideal work environments they have been describing? What factors are missing?

12. Give out the strips of coloured paper. Ask each student to write three positive steps they could take to make a better work environment for themselves.

13. Collect in the strips. Arrange them around the circular poster to make a flower/sun shape.

14. Tell students you will ask for feedback at a specified time (the next day/ after the weekend, etc.) on what they have done to improve their work environment.

15. If you want to document changes they have implemented, you could do this in the form of extra petals/rays on the flower/sun showing what each student has achieved. (If you are feeling artistic/fanciful you could also do this in the form of bees/butterflies around the flower!)

Worksheet 1 Favourite workplaces

1. I cannot cope with distraction. I need somewhere very quiet. I often work in the library: I like the feeling of being with other people who are working too.

2. I have to be alone – I can only work in my room at home. I can't even work in the library where it is fairly quiet – there are too many other people there moving around.

3. I need to vary where I work. I mostly work at my desk in my room but I get bored there after a while. So one way I vary it is to go and work in a café for a bit. I like the background noise – but also I feel if I go there and pay for a coffee then I have to do some work!! I have to choose what I do in each place though – if it's something quite easy I can go to a café, but if it really needs concentration I need to have peace and privacy.

4. I mostly need to work at a desk but if I get stressed I go and work in the park. It's quiet and calm and green there and I can sit under a tree and feel really relaxed. Sometimes I go there if I am having difficulty learning or understanding something and I find the peace and quiet and mental space helps!

Worksheet 2 Ratings

Use this worksheet to rate the workplaces from 1 to 5 for distraction and relaxation:

1 = least distracting → 5 = most distracting

1 = least relaxing   → 5 = most relaxing

Add any workplaces you use or can think of as possibilities

Place	Distraction	Relaxation
Desk in your room		
Library		
Living room sofa		
Kitchen table		
Garden		
Park		

Activity 58: With a Little Help from my Friends

Aim: To get students to identify ways in which friends or family could help them to study

Level: Intermediate up

Time: 25 minutes

Materials: 'Help from my friends' worksheet, arrows, target poster

Preparation: Copy worksheet for each student, make 'Target' poster on large sheet of paper, make cut-out arrows on coloured paper for each student

Language practice	
Functions	making suggestions, talking about possibilities
Skills	reading, speaking, writing
Language areas	could, would

Procedure

1. Prepare the target poster: write on the bull's-eye in the centre: 'Ways family and friends can help me study'. Prepare the arrows. Copy a 'Help from my friends' worksheet for each student.

2. Put up the target on the wall. Use it to introduce the topic and ask students for any initial suggestions on how family or friends could help them study.

3. Give students the 'Help from my friends' worksheet. Ask them to read it and number the statements.

4. Put students in pairs or small groups to discuss what arrangements would work for them.

5. Put them in fours to brainstorm any other ideas they could add.

6. Get each group to produce a 'Hints and tips' sheet with study advice on how friends and family could help.

7. Pin these up round the room. Get students to go round the room with paper and pen and make notes of any ideas they could put into action in their own situations.

8. Give out the arrows. Ask students to write their action points in the arrows.

9. Pin up the arrows round the target.

10. Follow up after an interval with a discussion on what they have done and how it is working.

Worksheet 1 Help from my friends

Read the quotations and number them:

(1) = an agreement that stops you distracting yourself

(2) = an agreement that stops other people distracting you

(3) = an agreement to check up on achievement

- I give my mum my mobile phone and iPod when I start studying so that I'm not tempted!

- I have a bargain with my kid brother – if he doesn't come and annoy me when I'm studying, I'll play Uno with him. He'll do anything for a game of Uno!

- Our favourite TV programme is just when I need to be studying. Everyone in my family would be watching it and laughing, so I never had the motivation to be on my own studying. Now we have agreed to record it and watch it together.

- My flatmates and I all have a pact – we have to pay a fine if we check Facebook when we're meant to be studying. We put the money in a pot and use it to pay the phone bill. So of course if you check Facebook when you should be working you end up paying for most of the phone bill!

- We all got on each others' nerves in our flat because we never worked at the same time so I would be trying to work when other people had friends round. Now we have agreed a time when we can work and other times when we can make as much noise as we like.

- My friend and I have a contract with each other: once a week we have a quick meeting to check how we did. It really helps knowing that you are going to have to tell someone else how much study you did!

Worksheet 2 Target and arrow

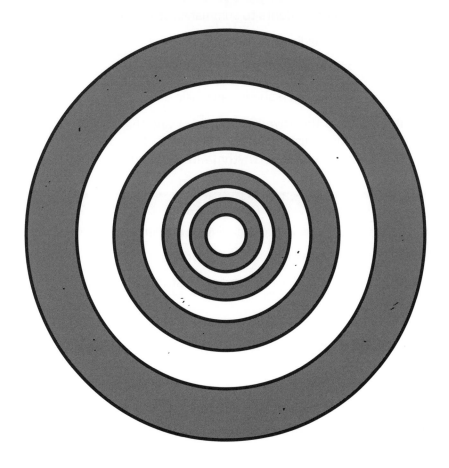

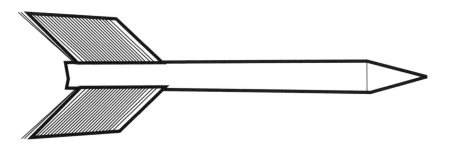

Photocopying of this worksheet is permitted: enlarge as necessary
© Jill Hadfield and Zoltán Dörnyei 2013

Activity 59: Strategies Rap

Aim:	To get students to summarise strategies in musical form
Level:	Intermediate up
Time:	25 minutes
Materials:	Rhymes worksheet, rap music CD
Preparation:	Copy the 'rhymes' worksheet and the 'strategies and techniques' list for each group of 3–4 students. Find a rap or preferably a rap rhythm without words

Language practice

Functions	various depending on students' creation
Skills	reading, speaking, writing
Language areas	various depending on students' creation

Procedure

1. Copy the rhymes worksheet for each group of 3–4 students. Bring the rap to class.

2. Play the rap and give the students the rhymes worksheet and the strategies list.

3. Ask them to brainstorm a possible two-liner for the first strategy: Defining expectations. Collect suggestions and put variations on the board.

4. Put students in groups and ask them to try to make one or more two-line raps.

5. Collect suggestions and put them together to make a complete rap.

Variation: letter to a future student

Elicit the strategies you have discussed and tried out with students in class. Put these up on the board or give students the strategies list.

1. Get students in pairs to discuss which strategies they found most useful.

2. Ask students to write a letter to a future student saying which strategies they tried and which they could recommend.

Worksheet 1 Strategies and techniques

- Define your expectations
- Give yourself rewards
- Eliminate distractions
- Use time management
- Vary your workplace
- Add humour and imagination
- Practise relaxation
- Cultivate optimism
- Organise your work environment
- Get cooperation from friends

Worksheet 2 Rhymes

Expectations	Reward	Distraction	Imagination
Situation	Applaud	Action	Frustration
Activation	Afford	Inaction	Creation
Motivation	Skateboard	Satisfaction	Dedication
Dedication		Attraction	Exploration
Education			Stimulation
Application			
Management	**Workplace**	**Optimism**	**Organisation**
Encouragement	Mental space	Dynamism	Realisation
Variation	**Relaxation**	**Cooperation**	
Recreation	Vacation	Transformation	
Inspiration	Liberation	Temptation	

Section 4: From strategies to achievement

What is meant by 'from strategies to achievement'?

This is the final stage in the route from vision to reality. It entails making your study intentions public and charting progress towards your long-term goal.

Why is it important to do this?

Making intentions public puts you under an obligation to fulfil them and thus increases motivation to achieve them. If they remain private there is less incentive to reach your goals. Charting progress is another way of increasing motivation – it is satisfying to know that you have come some way towards achieving your goal and it is a public validation of effort. Research has demonstrated that the way students feel about past accomplishments and the amount of satisfaction they experience on successful task completion will significantly determine how they approach subsequent learning tasks.

What does this entail?

The first part of Section 4 is concerned with making *learning contracts* between the class and the teacher and between pairs of students, in which intentions are written down and witnessed. The second half of the section contains activities that provide a public or private record of progress and thus validate effort.

What, therefore, is the aim of this section?

The aim of this section is to increase learner motivation through charting progress and rewarding effort.

How can this best be translated into practice in terms of usable classroom activities?

The first half of Section 4 involves the drawing up of a list of study intentions in the form of a contract which can then be witnessed at the start of the study plan and evaluated at the end. The second half involves different visual ways of keeping a record of progress.

Does this involve any issues and problems?

One issue is that of reward; whether rewards should be offered and whether these should reward performance or effort. Another issue is how public the contracts and the progress records should be made.

How can these issues best be dealt with?

Research indicates that feedback is an important factor in student motivation and that success in achieving goals should be attributed to effort rather than ability (i.e. saying 'Good job!' rather than saying 'Clever boy!'). The question of rewards has been a vexed one. In some cases rewards, and especially grades, can be detrimental to motivation, encouraging students to become too focused on them (i.e. become 'grade-grubbing') or to see their own self-worth only in terms of the grades they receive, particularly when they compare themselves unfavourably to others and thus lose motivation as a result. However, the rewarding of individual or class effort and success in achieving study intentions does not have to result in a process of grading and comparison – there is a delicate line to tread here.

With regard to the activities aimed at charting progress, they can be kept either as a private record or as a public statement of progress. It may be better to let individual students keep private progress records which you can validate from time to time, and have a public record of the progress of the class as a whole.

How can I best use these activities in my classroom to achieve the aim of this section?

Activities in the first part of Section 4 should be used before those in the second. It would make sense in general to prepare the contracts made at the beginning of the week, and the progress record updated at the end.

How much time you allocate to these activities depends on the constraints of your timetable and curriculum. However, research does indicate that feedback on successful task completion is a very important factor in increasing motivation to continue and go forward, and therefore you may consider allocating a regular time slot to this throughout your course. Once students are familiar with the process of making learning contracts with each other and of charting progress, these are activities which could be done outside class, but with a regular class slot for feedback.

Note: In Part III there is more advice on integrating activities into a course and adapting them to different levels and other contexts.

Activity 60: Study Buddies

Aim: To initiate a discussion on ways in which students can help each other study in and out of class

Level: Intermediate up

Time: 15 minutes

Materials: Brainstorm worksheet

Preparation: Make one copy of the Brainstorm sheet for each student

Language practice	
Functions	discussing possibilities
Skills	reading, writing, speaking
Language areas	could, would, if . . .

Procedure

1. Make a copy of the 'Brainstorm' sheet and give one to each student.

2. Ask them to work individually on the worksheet.

3. Put them in pairs to discuss their ideas and to generate more.

4. Put the pairs in fours to compile a list of all their ideas.

5. Prepare a checklist based on students' answers to the brainstorm; also include ideas of your own. Some ideas to include:

   - making study contracts and giving each other feedback
   - testing each other on vocabulary and grammar
   - listening to authentic material (e.g. films, TV programmes) together
   - having a conversation hour.

6. Make a copy of the checklist and give one to each student.

7. Ask them to work individually to tick the ways they feel would be most helpful for them.

8. Get students to identify who they would be happy to work with as a 'study buddy'. It is important to do this in a way that avoids the old school

practice of picking for teams where individuals may get left out or isolated. One way of doing this could be to ask students to get into fours with people they feel they could work with, then ask the fours to divide themselves into pairs. Another way is to ask each student to write the names of four or more people in the class they would be happy to work with. Collect these in and use this as a basis for assigning pairs. A further way is to ask students to write a sociogram: a mindmap of who works well together in the class.

Worksheet 1 Brainstorm

Think about study activities in class and at home.

Which activities do you do best alone?

Which activities could a friend help you with?

Make two lists:

Activities I do best alone	**How a friend could help me**
• _____	• _____
• _____	• _____
• _____	• _____
• _____	• _____
• _____	• _____
• _____	• _____
• _____	• _____
• _____	• _____
• _____	• _____
• _____	• _____
• _____	• _____

Activity 61: Study Contracts

Aim: To get students to write individual or class contracts for the week's learning objectives, which a fellow student can then witness and monitor

Level: Intermediate up

Time: 15 minutes

Materials: Contract worksheets

Preparation: Make one copy of the individual study contract for each student and one class contract for the whole class.

Language practice	
Functions	identifying aims and objectives
Skills	reading, writing
Language areas	going to, will

Procedure

1. Make a copy of the contract form for each student.

2. Get them to fill it in individually for the week ahead.

3. Get them to team up with their study buddy.

4. Students witness each other's contracts and make a date to give each other feedback.

5. You can also make a contract for the week's classwork and homework that you set which will be monitored and signed by you. An example form for this is given in Worksheet 2.

Worksheet 1 Individual study contract

This is what I hope to achieve this week:

This week in class we will:

For homework we will:

For self-study I will:

This is how I hope to do it:

	Mon	Tues	Wed	Thurs	Fri	Sat	Sun
Classwork							
Homework							
Self-study							

Signed: _____

Witnessed: _____

Date and time for feedback: _____

Worksheet 2 Class contract: week . . .

This week our goal is:

In order to achieve this we will do the following things:

In class we will:

For homework we will:

In addition, my personal goal this week is:

Name   *Goal*

Signed   _____

Witnessed   _____

Activity 62: Rate Yourself

Aim: To get students to rate their week's performance

Level: Intermediate up

Time: 15 minutes

Materials: Contract form from Activity 61

Preparation: None

Language practice

Functions	evaluating performance, giving reasons
Skills	reading, writing
Language areas	adverbs of degree, because

Procedure

1. Introduce students to a ratings scheme for assessing performance. An example is given below.

2. Get students to go through the learning contract they made for the week and rate each objective on the scale. They can do this in class or in their own time.

3. Pair them up with their study buddy and get them to go through how they rated their performance and give each other feedback – again this can be done in class or in their own time.

Example rating scheme

Rate your performance using this scale:

5 = I did this very well.

4 = I feel I achieved this objective.

3 = I did this quite well but need to do more work on this.

2 = I did not do this very well and need to revise this thoroughly.

1 = I did not do this at all and need to plan this in for next time.

Activity 63: Progress Ladders

Aim: To provide students with a way of charting progress and validating achievement

Level: Intermediate up

Time: 15 minutes

Materials: Progress ladder worksheet

Preparation: Make one copy of the progress ladder for each student.

Language practice	
Functions	recording achievement
Skills	writing
Language areas	past simple

Procedure

1. Make a copy of the progress ladder for each student. The ladder should have as many rungs as weeks in the course.

2. Give out the ladders and explain that this is a way of individually recording achievement.

3. Students should fill in the rungs on the ladder each week recording the aims that they achieved.

Variation: routemap

1. Make a copy of the 'Symbols' worksheet for each student.

2. Explain that you are going to ask students to draw a map of their progress through the course. They will keep the map and add to it each week, showing how far they have come each week and what difficulties they met/what obstacles they overcame. Each map will be a personal individual creation based on their own experience of their learning that week.

3. Give out the symbol sheets and go through them.

4. Ask students to begin their map showing the first section of the route they have travelled.

Worksheet 1 Progress ladders

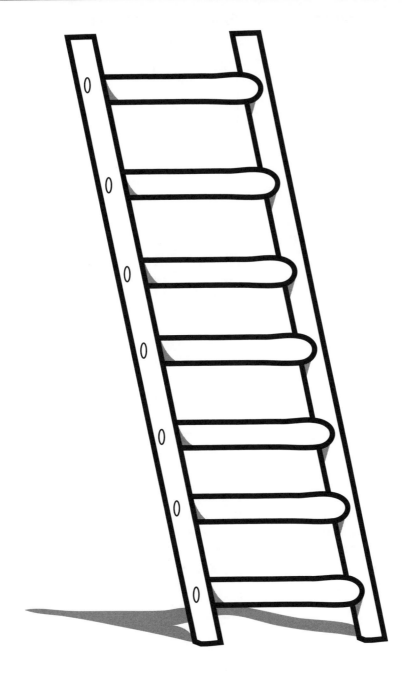

Worksheet 2 Symbols

Symbol	Meaning	Symbol	Meaning
	This was very difficult.		I got stuck!
	This was very easy.		I got bored.
	I achieved this easily.		I got muddled.
	There were some problems on the way.		I got distracted.
	I wasted time.		I enjoyed this.
	I had to revise this.		I deserved a rest/reward.

Activity 64: Contract Wall

Aim: To provide the class with a public way of charting progress through the course and validating achievement

Level: Intermediate up

Time: 15 minutes

Materials: Contracts as in Activity 61; wall poster

Preparation: Carry out Activity 61; make a wall poster.

Language practice	
Functions	recording achievement
Skills	writing
Language areas	past simple

Procedure

1. Make a wall poster. The poster should have as many bricks as weeks in the course. The bricks should be the same size as the contracts (see example below).

2. When you have completed the class contract for the week with the students, put up the wall poster and paste the contract on the first 'brick'.

3. At the end of the week get/give feedback as in Activity 61. If the majority of goals have been achieved – decide yourself what is a reasonable target – you could indicate in some way that the target has been met, perhaps by colouring in the brick or by sticking some coloured cellophane over it so that aims are still visible but the brick is coloured.

4. Continue the process each week.

5. If you like, you can offer class rewards for completion of aims (e.g. chocolate or biscuits for a satisfactory week) or a larger reward (e.g. watching a film) for a whole row of bricks. This will build a cooperative spirit and get students to work together to achieve class aims.

Variation 1: Contract tree

If you prefer, you can use the idea of a tree instead of a wall, with the trunk as the long-term goals, the branches as weekly goals and the contracts as fruit. This would entail making the week's class contracts in the shape of an apple, and colouring them red or green when achieved. Another possibility is a roadmap with the contracts as sections of the road, or a mountain with the contracts as flags on the way up.

Variation 2: Air balloon

1. Take a group photo of the class and get it enlarged (e.g. print it out and use a copier to enlarge it).

2. Make a balloon poster as in the sample below. There should be as many sections in the balloon as weeks in the course. Cut the group photo so that everyone's heads and shoulders appear in the basket. Put up the poster at ground level on a classroom wall.

3. Carry out the class contracts activity in Activity 61 with the students. (The contract should be the same size and shape as one of the sections of the balloon. It will also look better if you use coloured paper.) When you have completed the class contract for the week with the students, paste the contract on the first section of the balloon.

4. At the end of the week get/give feedback as in Progress Ladders (Activity 63). If the majority of goals have been achieved – decide yourself what is a reasonable target – you can raise the balloon a certain amount on the wall. Continue the process each week.

Example contract wall

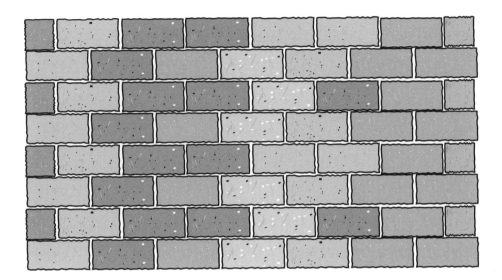

Example balloon poster

Activity 65: Progress Blog

Aim: To provide the class with an interactive way of charting and discussing progress through the course and validating achievement

Level: Intermediate up

Time: 15 minutes

Materials: Access to Internet

Preparation: Set up a wiki, discussion board or Ning website to which everyone can contribute

Language practice	
Functions	recording and evaluating achievement
Skills	writing
Language areas	past simple, adverbs of degree

Procedure

1. Set up a wiki, discussion board or ning and enrol all students and yourself as members.

2. Ask students to make an entry at the beginning of the first week, saying what their learning goals are for that week and what they aim to do to achieve them. At the beginning of subsequent weeks they can evaluate how they feel they did in the previous week and set goals and tasks for the week to come.

3. Students can view others' goals, plans and evaluations and comment (positively!).

4. From time to time look at students' entries and comment on them, giving encouragement and advice.

Chapter 3
Keeping the vision alive

It took me a long time to control my images and perfect my imagery, maybe a year, doing it every day. At first I couldn't see myself ... or I would see my dives wrong all the time. I would get an image of hurting myself, or tripping on the board ... As I continued to work at it, I got to the point where I could feel myself doing a perfect dive and hear the crowd yelling at the Olympics.

Gould, Damarjian and Greenleaf (2002: 70)

In this chapter, we return to the vision of the Future L2 Self created in Chapter 1. The aim here is to extend the vision and to deepen the sense of an L2 identity. Although this chapter follows Chapter 2 (Mapping the journey), the activities here are designed to be used in parallel with the goal-setting activities in that chapter, to appeal to the affective as well as the cognitive side of language learning and to keep the learner in touch with his/her initial vision.

We have taken two different paths towards the goal of keeping the vision alive: 'Developing identity' (Section 1) and 'Making it real' (Section 2). In the former, the aim is to keep in touch with the vision, to develop it in more detail and to make sure that it is not lost in the day-to-day business of doing grammar exercises and writing essays. 'Making it real' provides activities that allow for the use of the L2 in real-life, virtual or simulated situations, sending the students into the L2 community or bringing the L2 world into the classroom to make the language and culture come alive for the students.

Section 1 – 'Developing identity' – covers four themes:

- *Identity projects* contains projects aimed at developing and elaborating the L2 identity.

- *Targeted visualisations* contains more detailed and precisely targeted visualisations of the students coping successfully in various L2 situations.

- *Role models* provides the students with contact – in real life, through the web or through reading texts – of successful language learners to increase their awareness of what learning a language entails.

- *Self-belief* contains activities aimed at increasing the students' self-esteem and belief in their L2 selves.

Section 2 – 'Making it real' – focuses on three topics:

- *Entering the L2 community* contains activities aimed at getting students to interact with members of the L2 community, through sending students out into the community with projects and interview tasks, by inviting speakers into the classroom, or by setting up opportunities for online interaction through penpal schemes, networking sites and chat rooms.

- *Let's pretend* contains classroom activities which simulate interactions with the L2 community.

- *Cultural events* contains suggestions for bringing aspects of the L2 culture to life through classroom or extracurricular activities.

These multiple pathways share the goal of establishing a sense of the future L2 self that is elaborate and detailed and which is reinforced by experience and understanding of the L2 community.

Section 1: Developing identity

What is meant by 'developing identity'?

'Developing identity' means working with the learners in a number of ways to develop and extend the vision of the L2 self initiated in Chapter 1: 'Imaging identity'.

Why is it important to do this?

It is important to do this for several reasons: in order to keep learners in touch with their original motivating vision of the L2 self, to enrich and extend that vision so that it is not just static but a living, growing entity, and to provide activities for the affective side of language learning to complement the cognitive goal setting activities in Chapter 2.

What does developing identity entail?

It entails providing activities which give the learner the opportunity to add to and deepen the initial vision, and to visualise precise situations in the L2 in more detail, and providing inspiration through role models to enhance learners' self-esteem and belief that they have the capability to attain their vision.

What, therefore is the aim of this section?

The aim of this section is to develop and enrich the vision of the Ideal L2 Self and to keep it at the forefront of learners' minds.

How can this best be translated into practice in terms of usable classroom activities?

There are four sub-sections, each taking a different path to developing the sense of L2 identity:

- *Identity projects* contains projects aimed at developing and elaborating the L2 identity, through activities such as writing a letter from the future self, creating a future self photo album and expressing identity through Bebo pages and the Internet-based online virtual world of 'Second Life'. Many of these activities are projects which can be extended each week as the sense of self is built up.

- *Targeted visualisations* contains more detailed and precisely targeted visualisations of the students coping successfully in various L2 situations. It is of course impossible to provide visualisations for all L2 situations, but four examples are given for the areas of 'goods and services', 'social life', 'work' and 'study', with templates to follow to create more visualisations for each area.

- *Role models* provides the students with contact – in real life, through the web or through reading texts – of successful language learners to increase their awareness of what learning a language entails. Activities in this section include a webquest, listening comprehension, jigsaw reading and interviews.

- *Self-belief* contains activities aimed at increasing students' self-esteem and belief in their abilities as L2 learners through activities such as 'Secret Friends', 'Affirmation Sheets', compliment claiming and self-adverts.

Does this involve any issues and problems and how can these best be dealt with?

Time factors may prove a problem in implementing these activities. You will need to select activities carefully to fit in with the demands of your syllabus. Many activities can be done for homework, many involve a very small amount of time (e.g. 'Claim a Compliment!' or 'Targeted Visualisations') and all have a language learning aim so that activities can be chosen to fulfil the dual role of increasing motivation and language practice.

How can I best use these activities in my classroom to achieve the aim of this section?

Activities should be done concurrently and spread throughout the term. You could select, for example, an identity project, such as creating an L2 Bebo page, and do this as ongoing project work with time allocation in class or for homework. Role models can be treated in a similar way with students working to compile an advice booklet consisting of strategies they find helpful from reading about or listening to successful language learners. Targeted visualisations can be done before activities such as roleplay or simulation to act as 'rehearsals' and to boost students' confidence. Other confidence-boosting activities can be done on a regular basis if they do not require much time (e.g. 'Secret Friends' or 'Claim a Compliment!') or, alternatively, can be saved to raise morale at points where students are flagging.

Note: In Part III there is more advice on integrating activities into a course and adapting them to different levels and other contexts.

Identity projects

Activity 66: Board Game

Aim:	To clarify some of the opportunities and pitfalls aiding or impeding progress to the ideal future self
Level:	Pre-intermediate up
Time:	20 minutes
Materials:	Board Game worksheet
Preparation:	Make one copy of the board game diagram for each student (or pair of students if you prefer).

Language practice	
Functions	describing situations, giving instructions
Skills	speaking, writing
Language areas	present simple, imperatives

Procedure

1. Give a copy of the board game diagram to each student (or pair of students if you prefer).

2. Ask them to imagine the board as a journey from their present self towards their goal of the future L2 self.

3. Ask them to fill in the squares with opportunities, pitfalls and achievements on the way; for example:

   • Pitfalls: 'You have an important assignment. You planned to finish it this evening but you spent too much time on Facebook. Miss a go.'

   • Opportunities: 'You decide to use the time spent waiting for the bus on memorising your vocabulary cards. Move forward one square.'

   • Achievements: 'Congratulations! You gave a talk about your hobbies in class today. Have another go!'

4. When they have finished get them to compare games with other students, or pairs of students.

5. Make a class display of the games.

Worksheet 1 Board Game

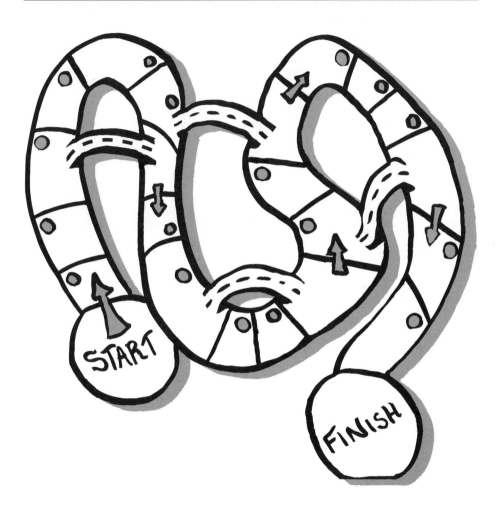

Activity 67: Letter from My Future Self

Aim: To recognise the hard work that goes into achieving the ideal L2 self.

Level: Pre-intermediate up

Time: Two periods of 20 minutes each

Materials: Reading quest worksheet

Preparation: Collect in students' letters; prepare and copy the 'Find some-one who . . .' reading quest worksheet

Language practice	
Functions	describing situations, thanking
Skills	writing, reading
Language areas	present simple, present continuous, present perfect, thank you for -ing

Procedure

1. Ask students to imagine their ideal self in the future. In their imagination, they should move forward in time so that they *are* their ideal self. Now ask them to think back about the past and the journey taken to get to their vision. What things helped to achieve their goal? What did they do to help their self-journey?

2. Ask them to write a thank you letter from their future self to their present self to express gratitude for all the things (hard work, good study habits, overcoming shyness, etc.) that helped them on their way.

3. Collect in the letters and for the next lesson prepare a reading quest:

   - Pin the letters up around the walls and give each a letter, A, B, C, etc.
   - Write a 'Find someone who . . .' reading quest; see sample worksheet below.
   - Get students to walk around the class, reading the texts and identify-ing them by writing the appropriate letter next to each question.

Worksheet 1 'Find someone who . . .' reading quest

Find someone who . . .	Name
worked hard on overcoming shyness and tried to speak more in class	
increased their vocabulary by reading books and newspapers outside class	
memorised the lyrics of (L2) . . . songs	
etc.	

Activity 68: Future Photo Albums

Aim: To create a tangible 'product' for display as a follow-up activity to Activity 30 in Section 5 on 'Enhancing the vision'

Level: Pre-intermediate up

Time: A short time allocation each week over several weeks

Materials: Paper, camera, props

Preparation: Do Activity 30 (Future Photo Album) in Section 5.

Language practice	
Functions	describing situations
Skills	writing, reading, speaking
Language areas	present continuous

Procedure

1. Do Activity 30 (Future Photo Album) in Section 5 on 'Enhancing the vision'.

2. After students have 'shown' their imaginary albums to each other, get them to work in groups to discuss what props they would need to bring to class in order to take the photos they have described.

3. Get them to bring a camera and the props to class the next day and to take the photos, or set it as a homework assignment as they may want to take photos 'on location' (e.g. talking round a table in someone's house, shopping in a market, in a café, etc.).

4. Get them to produce future photo albums with descriptions written for each photo.

5. Display the albums.

6. You can do this activity as a 'one-off' activity or as an ongoing project with students adding a photo each week, as they learn more language.

Activity 69: Future Diaries

Aim: Students maintain an ongoing reflective diary – not on past experiences but on future visions

Level: Pre-intermediate up

Time: A slot each week for homework

Materials: None

Preparation: None

Language practice	
Functions	describing events, abilities and experiences, expressing feelings
Skills	writing, reading
Language areas	present simple, present perfect, can/could, past simple

Procedure

1. Introduce students to the idea of a 'future diary'. Begin by using one of the future self visualisations you have done as a basis. Ask students to reflect on what they have said or written, and to discuss in pairs what might be the first step in the process.

2. Get them to write an imaginary diary entry for that step for a day in the future.

3. Create a display of diary entries, or get students to create a blog that others can read.

4. Continue on an ongoing basis: as students acquire more language and skills get them to add diary entries about their future abilities and experiences.

Activity 70: L2 Self Bebo/Facebook Pages

Aim: To get students to create an interactive L2 identity

Level: Pre-intermediate up

Time: A short time allocation in class or for homework every week

Materials: None

Preparation: None

Language practice	
Functions	personal information, abilities, feelings, narration of experience
Skills	writing, reading
Language areas	mixed tenses, modals

Procedure

1. Arrange a session – in the computer lab if possible, or on laptops, or get students to do this at home – where students can set up a Bebo or Facebook page for their future L2 self identity. (Facebook is more popular but Bebo has more possibilities for idiosyncratic expression of identity.)

2. Get students to create a 'skin' and start a profile of their future L2 self, perhaps adding photos from the album they have created if you have done Activity 68.

3. Create some time each week in class or for homework where students can access each other's Bebo pages and add comments.

Activity 71: 'Second Life'

Aim: To get students to create an interactive L2 identity

Level: Pre-intermediate up

Time: A short time allocation in class or for homework every week

Materials: None

Preparation: None

Language practice	
Functions	personal information, abilities, feelings, narration of experience
Skills	writing, reading
Language areas	mixed tenses, modals

Procedure

1. Set up a session – in the computer lab if possible, if not, on laptops, or get students to do this at home – where students can log into the Internet-based online virtual world of 'Second Life'.

2. Get students to create an avatar of their future L2 self.

3. Create some time each week in class or for homework where students can interact with each other in the L2 through 'Second Life'.

Targeted visualisations

Activity 72: Goods and Services: In a Restaurant

Aim:	To visualise the L2 self ordering meals in the L2
Level:	Pre-intermediate up
Time:	20 minutes
Materials:	None
Preparation:	Rehearse the script

Language practice	
Functions	describing actions and feelings
Skills	listening, speaking
Language areas	can, present simple, present perfect, past simple + vocabulary for food and drink, vocabulary for feelings

Procedure

1. If you like, play some soft background music.

2. Ask learners to close their eyes. Tell them you are going to ask them to imagine themselves in a restaurant in an L2-speaking country, speaking the L2.

3. Begin asking the questions from the script, allowing time between each question for learners to imagine themselves in the scenario you 'dictate'.

4. When you have finished, ask learners to open their eyes and share their vision with the person sitting next to them.

5. Round off the activity by asking each learner to say something to the group about how they felt.

Script

Imagine . . . you are in (a foreign country) . . . you are walking along a street with a friend . . . who are you with? . . . it is evening and you are going to a restaurant – what kind of restaurant have you chosen? . . . what does the street look like? . . . what can you see around you? . . . is it crowded? . . . what is the weather like? . . .

You reach the restaurant and go in . . . what does the restaurant look like? . . . is it full? . . . is it noisy or quiet? . . . is there music? . . . what can you smell?

The waiter shows you to a table and gives you the menu . . . you read the menu and understand it . . . what is on it? . . . you translate for your friend . . . what have you decided to have? . . . the waiter comes over and you order the meal . . . he nods and writes everything down . . . you have ordered a meal successfully in (L2) . . . how do you feel?

Variations

It is of course possible to provide similar visualisations before any simulation – and equally impossible to provide them all here! Below is a template for creating your own visualisations for simulations involving goods and services such as the ones in this chapter.

Visualisation template

(1) Set the scene

Typical instructions:

- Imagine you are . . . (e.g. in an airport, shopping centre, in someone's house).
- You are . . . -ing (e.g. you are shopping for a dinner party).
- You have just . . . (e.g. you have just come off a flight from Santiago).

(2) Get learners to imagine more concrete details of the scene vividly

Typical questions:

- Are you with anyone?
- What can you see?
- What can you hear?
- What can you smell?
- How do you feel?
- Is it . . . or . . . ?

(3) Introduce the task

Sample instructions:

- You would like to . . .
- You are going to . . . (e.g. cook, watch, buy, etc.).
- You need to get . . .
- You have lost your . . . , you need to find it . . .
- The telephone rings and you answer it . . . it's your . . .

(4) Imagine success with the task

Sample instructions:

- You ask for what you want . . .
- The shopkeeper understands you . . .
- You understand the price . . .
- You ask a question and receive the needed information . . .
- They understand you and tell you to wait . . .
- They find your luggage . . .
- You understand everything and are able to reply fluently . . .
- You succeed in . . .

(5) Celebrate success

Typical question:

- How do you feel?

Activity 73: Social: At a Party

Aim: To visualise the L2 self interacting successfully with strangers at a party

Level: Pre-intermediate up

Time: 20 minutes

Materials: None

Preparation: Rehearse the script

Language practice	
Functions	describing actions and feelings
Skills	listening, speaking
Language areas	can, present simple, present perfect, past simple, vocabulary for feelings

Procedure

1. If you like, play some soft background music.

2. Ask learners to close their eyes. Tell them you are going to ask them to imagine themselves at a party, speaking the L2.

3. Begin asking the questions from the script, allowing time between each question for learners to imagine themselves in the scenario you 'dictate'.

4. When you have finished, ask learners to open their eyes and share their vision with the person sitting next to them.

5. Round off the activity by asking each learner to say something to the group about how they felt.

Script

Imagine . . . you have been invited to a party . . . there are a lot of (L2) . . . speakers there . . . what is the room like? . . . how many people are there? . . . is there music? . . . is there food? . . . you don't know many people . . . how do you feel?

Imagine some of the people . . . imagine one person coming up to start a conversation in (L2) . . . they introduce themselves and you reply . . . you start talking about where you come from . . . where you live . . . what you do . . . hobbies and interests . . . some past experiences . . . they understand you and you can talk fluently . . . how do you feel?

They then introduce you to another friend . . . and you start talking . . .

Note: For a general visualisation template that you can use to create other scripts, please see Activity 72.

Activity 74: Work: Job Interview

Aim: To visualise the L2 self having a job interview in the L2

Level: Pre-intermediate up

Time: 20 minutes

Materials: None

Preparation: Rehearse the script

Language practice	
Functions	describing actions and feelings
Skills	listening, speaking
Language areas	can, present simple, present perfect, past simple, vocabulary for feelings, vocabulary for personal qualities

Procedure

1. If you like, play some soft background music.

2. Ask learners to close their eyes. Tell them you are going to ask them to imagine themselves having a job interview, speaking the L2.

3. Begin asking the questions from the script, allowing time between each question for learners to imagine themselves in the scenario you 'dictate'.

4. When you have finished, ask learners to open their eyes and share their vision with the person sitting next to them.

5. Round off the activity by asking each learner to say something to the group about how they felt.

Script

Imagine ... you are having a job interview in (foreign country) ... you are waiting outside the office at the moment but you do not feel nervous ... you feel relaxed ... calm and confident ... now they have called you to go in ... what is the office like? ...

There are three people at a table ... what are they like? ... you sit down opposite them ... still feeling calm and confident ... the people smile and introduce themselves . . . they seem very friendly . . . you begin to feel you would like to work here . . .

They begin to ask you questions about yourself . . . why you are applying for the job . . . what experience you have had . . . how you think you can contribute . . . what you have to offer . . . you answer confidently and fluently . . . the atmosphere is quite relaxed and you are getting on well . . . at the end you shake hands . . . and they offer you the job . . . how do you feel?

Note: For a general visualisation template that you can use to create other scripts, please see Activity 72.

Activity 75: Study and Exams: Giving a Presentation

Aim: To visualise the L2 self giving a successful class presentation

Level: Pre-intermediate up

Time: 20 minutes

Materials: None

Preparation: Rehearse the script

Language practice	
Functions	describing actions and feelings
Skills	listening, speaking
Language areas	can, present simple, present perfect, past simple, vocabulary for feelings

Procedure

1. If you like, play some soft background music.

2. Ask learners to close their eyes. Tell them you are going to ask them to imagine themselves at a conference in the foreign country, giving a presentation in the L2.

3. Begin asking the questions from the script, allowing time between each question for learners to imagine themselves in the scenario you 'dictate'.

4. When you have finished, ask learners to open their eyes and share their vision with the person sitting next to them.

5. Round off the activity by asking each learner to say something to the group about how they felt.

Script

Imagine . . . you have to give a conference presentation on . . . (choose topic or ask students to choose topic) . . . you are interested in the topic and have worked hard on preparing it . . .

You have a PowerPoint and pictures to show the audience . . . you are waiting for your turn . . . how is the lecture room arranged? . . . who is there? . . . where does the speaker stand? . . . you are feeling relaxed and confident about giving the talk.

Now it is your turn to speak . . . where are you standing? . . . who can you see? . . . the atmosphere in the room is quite relaxed . . . the people seem friendly . . . they are looking forward to your talk . . .

You begin . . . you speak fluently and confidently . . . you make good eye contact with your audience . . . your body language is confident . . . people seem interested in your topic . . . your talk is going well and everyone is enjoying it . . . you are enjoying speaking too . . . you make a joke and everyone laughs . . .

Now you have finished . . . you are sure you have done well and will get good feedback . . . how do you feel?

Note: For a general visualisation template that you can use to create other scripts, please see Activity 72.

Role models

Activity 76: Good Language Learners

Aim: To raise student awareness about what makes a good language learner

Level: Intermediate up

Time: 20–30 minutes

Materials: Small pieces of blank paper

Preparation: Prepare a pile of small pieces of blank paper for each pair of students

Language practice	
Functions	talking about habits and routines, describing feelings
Skills	writing, speaking
Language areas	present simple

Procedure

1. Put students in pairs and give each a pile of small pieces of blank paper.

2. Ask students the question: What makes a good language learner? Get them to write answers on the small pieces of paper – one idea per piece. They should do this individually without talking. Set a time limit, say five minutes.

3. At the end of the time limit, the pairs look at their pile of ideas and discuss. They can throw away any ideas that are duplicated to arrive at a pile of shared ideas.

4. Put the pairs in fours and repeat the process.

5. Now get the groups to turn the ideas into a series of questions. For example, if one of their ideas was 'Speak the L2 as much as possible outside class', they can make the question: 'How much do you speak (L2) outside class?' They should work so that each student ends up with a questionnaire to take from the group for the next stage.

6. Regroup the students so that the new groups contain one member from each of the old groups and get students to interview each other.

Activity 77: Interview a Role Model

Aim: To interview a successful language learner as a role model for students

Level: Intermediate up

Time: 20–30 minutes

Materials: Questionnaire

Preparation: Make copies of the questionnaire for students; give one to the speaker in advance

Language practice	
Functions	talking about habits and routines, describing feelings
Skills	writing, speaking
Language areas	present simple

Procedure

1. Make copies of the questionnaire for the students, and give one to the speaker in advance.

2. Before the speaker comes, go through the questionnaire with the students. You can allocate questions for them to ask, or interview the speaker yourself and allow time at the end for student questions.

3. Interview the speaker. Students take notes on the questionnaire.

4. Give them time to ask their own questions at the end.

5. After the speaker has left, put students in groups to discuss what they found helpful.

6. Ask the groups to report back to the class.

Note: This activity lends itself to being followed up by Activity 79.

Worksheet 1 Successful language learner's questionnaire

You are obviously a successful language learner! Congratulations!

1. Which foreign languages do you speak?

2. Which do you speak best?

3. How did you begin learning the language?

4. What made you want to continue?

5. What kept you going through difficult patches?

6. If you had a vision of yourself as a future user of the language, what was this?

7. Did you have any effective ways of . . .

    a. setting goals for yourself?

    b. breaking the goals down?

    c. studying?

8. A Hungarian proverb says: 'You are as many people as the languages you speak.' When you speak a foreign language, do you feel like a different person in some way? How?

9. Do you feel speaking another language adds anything to your life? What?

Activity 78: Webquest

Aim:	To carry out a Webquest on what makes a successful language learner
Level:	Intermediate up
Time:	45 minutes
Materials:	Webquest worksheets
Preparation:	Check the addresses on the Webquest worksheet first to make sure they have not gone out of date and add new ones to each Webquest; make copies of each Webquest for half the class.

Language practice

Functions	expressing likes and preferences
Skills	writing, speaking
Language areas	present simple

Procedure

1. Copy updated Webquests 1 and 2, each for half your class.

2. Give half the students Webquest 1 and the other half Webquest 2.

3. Get them to carry out the Webquest, listing the various characteristics of a successful language learner.

4. When they have finished, put them in pairs to share their information. Give them three questions:

   • Do the successful language learners interviewed on the sites on Webquest 1 agree with the general advice given on the sites in Webquest 2?

   • What points are most commonly mentioned?

   • What advice do you find most helpful?

Worksheet 1 Webquest 1

What makes a good language learner?

Browse these interviews with successful language learners and make a list of all the points they mention.

Do the language learners agree over what makes a successful learner?

Which points are mentioned most often?

Which advice do you find helpful?

Interviews

www3.telus.net/linguisticsissues/successful.html

http://blog lenguajero.com/successful-language-learners-interview-with-sara-elaine-magil/

http://blog.lenguajero.com/successful-language-learners-interview-with-john-biesnecker/

http://toshuo.com/2009/interviews-with-successful-language-learners/

Worksheet 2 Webquest 2

What makes a good language learner?

Browse these lists of characteristics of good learners and make a list of all the points they mention.

Do the authors agree what makes a successful learner?

Which points are mentioned most often?

Which advice do you find helpful?

Summaries of characteristics of a good language learner

http://emp.byui.edu/tayloral1/the%20successful%20language%20learner.htm

http://webcache.googleusercontent.com/search?q=cache:zmlxf4v31uwj:www.omf.org/content/download/6886/33214/file/characteristics_of_good_learners.pdf+characteristics+good+language+learner&hl=en&gl=nz

www.language.com.hk/articles/goodll.html

Activity 79: Role Model Roleplay

Aim: To raise student awareness about what makes a good language learner

Level: Intermediate up

Time: 20–30 minutes

Materials: Reading texts and questionnaire

Preparation: Copy each reading text for half the class, copy the questionnaire from Activity 77 for everyone

Language practice	
Functions	talking about habits and routines, describing feelings
Skills	reading, speaking
Language areas	present simple

Procedure

1. Put students in two groups. Give out reading text A to Group A and text B to Group B.

2. Ask students to read the text and ask themselves the question: What can I learn from this person's experience? Allow some time for students to read the text then get them to discuss it in their group.

3. Regroup students in pairs so they are with a partner from a different group. Give copies of the questionnaire (from Activity 77) to everyone.

4. Students interview each other, asking the questions on the questionnaire, responding as if they are the person who wrote the text.

5. The pairs discuss what they found helpful and what strategies they could adopt themselves.

Text A Successful language learner: German

Which foreign languages do you speak?

French, German, Italian, Spanish and Chinese

Which do you speak best?

German

How did you begin learning the language?

I studied German for two years in high school, then spent a year in Germany after school working in a kindergarten in a hospital. At university I did a diploma in German as my minor.

I feel I benefited from two very different ways of learning a language. The schoolwork was very traditional grammar-translation methodology with an emphasis on accuracy – nearly all reading and writing with very little speaking. When I worked in Germany, on the other hand, there was little reading and writing – only listening and speaking. And no one corrected me! Though I knew when I wasn't communicating successfully by the blank looks on people's faces! So this was a much more intuitive way of learning the language – just by 'picking it up' with the emphasis on fluency not accuracy. I paid no attention to grammar, but picked up 'chunks' of language, whole phrases and expressions, which I enjoyed inserting into what I was saying and which gave me the feeling of being 'authentic'! Sometimes I had not much idea of what these pieces of language actually meant. *Beziehungsweise* was one example. I could not have translated it, but from having heard it used so much, knew exactly how to use it and using it made me feel really 'German'. I feel I learned much more that way. But I wonder, though, how much I would have learned and how difficult it would have been, particularly in the initial stages, if I had not had that basic grounding in grammar.

What made you want to continue?

Getting a job in Germany between school and university.

What kept you going through difficult patches?

Wanting to communicate with people.

If you had a vision of yourself as a future user of the language, what was this?

I had a vision of myself as a fluent communicator, making friends and having meaningful conversations. I found it very exciting to be living abroad and having a sense of myself as a European. I felt that this was my adventurous self, also a more sophisticated self, a more intellectual self. The deep and meaningful conversations were definitely a part of my L2 self. I wanted to go to university in Germany (though ended up going back to Britain) so I suppose my future L2 self was a university student.

Do you have any effective ways of studying?

I had two different ways of learning. At school I was systematic about learning vocabulary and grammar; when I lived in Germany I just 'went with the flow' – just tried to speak and listen as much as possible, without being inhibited or afraid to try things out. At university I combined the two ways: I tried to do as much reading (stories, novels, newspapers) as possible – I found that reading a lot outside class really improved my vocabulary – and also to speak some German with German students to keep up my fluency, as well as the more formal classwork, which focused on translation and interpreting, where I went back to learning vocabulary and focusing more on accuracy – trying to learn from my mistakes.

A Hungarian proverb says: 'You are as many people as the languages you speak.' When you speak a foreign language, do you feel like a different person in some way? How?

My 'German Self'? Yes, very different from my English Self! Much more intense, intellectual, more given to theorising, more prone to abstractions. Less flippant, less ironic. It probably helped that I was about 19 at the time and in a university city with a strong café culture – full of intense late night discussions! Incidentally, my 'French self' is also more analytic and theoretical. It is possibly something of a combined 'Euroself' – no accident that both countries have a great tradition of philosophy.

Do you feel speaking another language adds anything to your life? What?

Definitely! It's like an extension of your personality, a window onto a different way of looking at the world.

Text B Successful language learner: French

Which foreign languages do you speak?

French, intermediate German, low-intermediate Russian (a long time ago), beginner Spanish, Mandarin, and basic Maori!!! Reading skills: Portuguese, Italian . . . sort of.

Which do you speak best?

French

How did you begin learning the language?

At kindergarten! Brilliant teacher who taught us a little French each day aged 3–4–5. I remember things in the classroom were labelled 'la fenêtre', 'la porte', etc.

Then I learned in a more formal way from the age of 8 at primary school. Inspiring teachers, including the 'senior' one who was a very good speaker, wore a beret, was kind and supportive. Very traditional grammar-translation text-based teaching, but he made it fun too, encouraging a bit of creativity – for those days perhaps revolutionary.

What made you want to continue?

Doing well at school I suppose, but also the fact that my father was a fluent French speaker (having attended Lausanne University in his twenties) and spoke French with business associates who frequently came to the house. We had a French girl or two staying (au pairs or school exchange) when I was aged 6–7–8. Ski trips to Switzerland – trains down through France with the multilingual signs. I was exposed to European languages as background noise through my early years – French, German (*Schweizerdeutsch*) and Italian. I used to mumble to myself in 'foreign language' when I was 9–10 pretending to be an international spy . . . Also in 1961–62 we had two family summer holidays in France and I remember being delighted to be understood talking to some fishermen landing their catch at Barfleur. Quite early – 14 or 15 – I decided that if I went to university, I'd like to follow my father and go to Lausanne . . . hopes dashed when the international fees were known but I think my father was encouraging – he thought languages would be as useful for 'business' as they had been to him.

What kept you going through difficult patches?

I suppose I was 'good at exams' and good at French, Latin, so it was not, as far as I can recall, ever a struggle . . . UNTIL I first went to France on my own and discovered that I could not easily order a drink in a café, even though I could read Racine in the original! This was a shock. And in Paris, after two years at university, I went to a film on my first night – couldn't understand a word (discovered at the end it was all in Quebecois!).

If you had a vision of yourself as a future user of the language, what was this?

- James Bond spy character able to use many languages perfectly (age 10 or so).

- Living in France and able to function 100% in French (from O Levels onwards, aged 16).

- Maybe transferring culture/nationality from British to French (I was very pro-European) (A levels onwards).

- Living and working in France.

Did you have any effective ways of studying?

Can't remember really – too long ago. Lots and lots of reading in schooldays obviously gave me a firm foundation in vocabulary, grammar, registers . . . Oral skills came later, inevitably, and I don't think I ever fully caught up (i.e. my writing + reading skills are stronger than my spoken and listening even though I have spent six plus years living in Francophone countries (France and Madagascar). I actively ENJOY using a dictionary and doing translations, so am good at 'small-scale' stuff as well as lengthier tasks (TV, cinema, discussions, reading novels). My schooling, and being good at Latin and French, means I do NOT find the sentence-level focus on fine grammar points boring at all – in fact that sort of work is my 'comfort zone' and interestingly where I feel 'safe' in my present attempts to learn Maori!

A Hungarian proverb says: 'You are as many people as the languages you speak.' When you speak a foreign language, do you feel like a different person in some way? How?

Yes, most definitely. It is a form of 'roleplay' or acting. My French is good enough for me to have had interesting conversations with many people at different stages of my life, and I even found I think different kinds of thoughts when 'in French' – more alert intellectually, more 'dialectic', more prone to take a hardline attitude to a problem (political, aesthetic, whatever). I find I enjoy arguing more in French than in English.

Do you feel speaking another language adds anything to your life? What?

Most definitely. The impression of crossing a threshold into a different culture, the opportunity to explore that culture as it were 'from the inside'. Like going into a cave and finding it full of light and fantastic new things to play with – maybe this is an image from *King Solomon's mines* (Rider Haggard). A very attractive proposition, stepping outside one's 'normal' (English) self and into a different role. Why this should be attractive I don't know – sounds very Freudian somehow!

Self-belief

Activity 80: Secret Friends

Aim:	To offer students affirmation from their peers to increase self-esteem
Level:	Pre-intermediate up, perhaps better with upper primary and secondary pupils
Time:	5 minutes to set up, thereafter 5 minutes on an ongoing basis to distribute mail
Materials:	Box with slit to act as post box
Preparation:	Have a post box in which students can post notes to their secret friends

Language practice	
Functions	giving praise
Skills	writing, reading
Language areas	past simple, positive adjectives and adverbs, e.g. well, fluently, great, confident, etc.

Procedure

1. Introduce the idea of 'secret friends': everyone in the class is secretly teamed up with a partner, who is their 'secret friend'. (If you like, you can give everyone in the class more than one secret friend – suggest 2 or 3 max.)

2. Get everyone to write their name on a slip of paper and put it in a bag. (If you are doing multiple secret friends get everyone to write their name twice or three times on different slips.)

3. Go round with the bag as a lucky dip. Each student takes one name (or two or three) from the bag. This is the name of your secret friend (if you get your own name, you should put it back of course). You must not disclose this name to anyone.

4. During the week that follows, students should write notes to their friends, praising them for things they did well, got better at or tried hard with. If you want to make sure everything is positive, keep a post box in the class and have certain times when 'post' is delivered. That way you can scan through the notes and make sure everything is positive.

5. At the end of term it is nice to have secret friend gifts – either set a (very low) price limit, or say it must be something they have made. (Some classes get so enthusiastic about secret friends that they start this custom spontaneously!)

Activity 81: Affirmation Sheets

Aim: To offer students affirmation from their peers to increase self-esteem

Level: Pre-intermediate up, perhaps better with upper primary and secondary pupils

Time: 1 hour or ongoing

Materials: Large sheet of paper for each student

Preparation: Write one student's name at the centre of each piece of paper

Language practice	
Functions	giving praise
Skills	writing, reading
Language areas	past simple, positive adjectives and adverbs, e.g. well, fluently, great, confident, etc.

Note: This is a good activity for the end of a term – or perhaps to cheer up a mid-term slump.

Procedure

1. Write a student's name at the centre of each sheet of paper. Give the sheets out randomly, ensuring that no one gets their own sheet of paper.

2. Get students to write affirmative messages on the sheet for each student in the class. When they have finished one student's sheet, they should pass it on to another student (but not the one whose name is on the sheet).

3. If you do not want to devote a lesson to this, you could organise it on an ongoing basis. One way of doing so would be to fold each sheet in quarters and write the students' names on the reverse side. Pin them up on a board. When students come in at the beginning of a class, or when they have some free time (e.g. in the break), they can take a sheet that they haven't contributed to, and write something on it.

Activity 82: Claim a Compliment!

Aim: To offer students affirmation to increase self-esteem

Level: Pre-intermediate up, perhaps better with upper primary and secondary pupils

Time: 10 minutes

Materials: OHT or PowerPoint slide

Preparation: Prepare an OHT or PowerPoint slide with a short message for each students saying something positive about their progress and ability (without naming them)

Language practice

Functions	giving praise
Skills	reading, speaking
Language areas	past simple, positive adjectives and adverbs, e.g. well, fluently, great, confident, etc.

Procedure

1. Put up the OHT or PowerPoint slide with the positive messages (but without any names) and ask students to work in groups to discuss which compliments they could claim.

2. Go through and get groups to report back.

Activity 83: New!! Exciting!!

Aim: To get students to write positive statements about their abilities and progress

Level: Pre-intermediate up, perhaps better with upper primary and secondary pupils

Time: 20 minutes

Materials: Advertisement poster template for each student, photo from each student

Preparation: Prepare a poster template for each student as in the example below get students to bring a photo of themselves to class

Language practice	
Functions	giving praise
Skills	writing, reading
Language areas	can, be able, positive adjectives and adverbs, e.g. well, fluently, hardworking, confident; comparatives, e.g. improved, better, etc.

Procedure

1. Give out the advertisement poster templates to each student and ask them to stick their photos in the space provided.

2. Get them to complete the advert with statements of the abilities and achievements they feel proud of. Under 'can' they write newly acquired abilities or proficiencies (e.g. can order meals in a restaurant, can have conversations on films, book and politics), under 'is' they write positive adjectives about their abilities (e.g. confident, willing to try, hard working). Under 'new design features', they write areas in which they feel they have made/are making progress (e.g. improved concentration, increased confidence, fewer mistakes).

3. Display the adverts!

4. You can repeat this at different points in the year.

Worksheet 1 New!! Exciting!!

frame for
photo

Class X brings you the latest model of _____(L2) speaker:

_____ (space for name or invented name)!

_____ can:

_____ is:

Unique new design features include:

Get one today! You will be delighted!

Section 2: Making it real

What is meant by 'making it real'?

'Making it real' means creating real life L2 situations for the students, giving them an opportunity to experience the culture and customs of the L2 and to reflect on the differences between L1 and L2 culture.

Why is it important to make it real?

It is important to give the students opportunities of real-life situations in order to try out their L2 identity and reinforce their sense of self. These real-life situations and exposure to cultural events and situations will help to make learning an L2 a living experience for the students and the opportunity of reflecting on cultural differences will help them understand and empathise with the culture. They will also allow them to add realistic details to their future L2 self visions.

What does 'making it real' entail?

It entails providing activities that allow for the use of the L2 in real life (virtual or simulated situations), sending the students into the L2 community or bringing the L2 world into the classroom to make the language and culture come alive for the students.

What, therefore, is the aim of this section?

The aim of the section is to provide students with experience of real-life L2 situations, opportunities to interact with L2 speakers, experience of culture and customs, and time to reflect on cultural difference in order to give them the chance to try out their L2 selves, and to understand and empathise with the L2 culture.

How can this best be translated into practice in terms of usable classroom activities?

This section focuses on three themes:

- *Entering the L2 community* contains activities aimed at getting students to interact with members of the L2 community, through sending students out into the community with projects and interview tasks, by inviting speakers into the classroom or by setting up opportunities for online interaction through e-pal schemes, networking sites and chat rooms.

- *Simulations* contains classroom activities which simulate interactions with the L2 community.

- *Cultural events* contains suggestions for bringing aspects of the L2 culture to life through classroom or extracurricular activities such as film screenings, cookery and festivals.

Does this involve any issues and problems?

One immediate problem is that entering the L2 community is likely to be more difficult if you are not teaching in an L2 country! Another problem is the case of English as an International Language. Students learning English may be learning the language to communicate with other L2 learners of English or as a means to an end (e.g. passing an exam) rather than through a desire to understand the culture of any one English-speaking country.

How can these issues best be dealt with?

Even if you are not teaching in the L2 speaking country, it may be possible to invite some L2 speakers into your classroom, or employ some L2 speakers in a chatroom (real, not virtual!). If this is not possible, you can use online resources such as networking sites, Internet chat rooms and e-pal sites to provide international interaction for your students. Simulations are also a way of making L2 situations realistic.

In the case of English as an International Language, it is possibly even more important to be aware of a range of cultural differences – a Swedish businessman may find himself communicating in English with a Japanese businessman one day and a Kenyan the next!

How can I best use these activities in my classroom to achieve the aim of this section?

The activities will fit into the syllabus in different ways. Simulations cover a range of situations commonly found in coursebooks and in the curriculum, and can easily be integrated into language work. The activities in 'Entering the L2 community' can form an ongoing project to develop speaking and listening skills, while the activities in 'Cultural events' can form occasional one-off break-the-routine lessons.

Note: In Part III there is more advice on integrating activities into a course and adapting them to different levels and other contexts.

Entering the L2 community

Activity 84: Projects: What to do in . . .

Aim: To make a short video as an introduction to new students on what to do in the town where the students are studying

Level: Pre-intermediate up

Time: Requires project time allocation over a number of weeks, or could be set as homework

Materials: Video camera(s), task sheet

Preparation: Make copies of the task sheet

Language practice	
Functions	talking about entertainment and leisure time
Skills	listening, speaking
Language areas	as required

Procedure

1. Make copies of the task sheet and cut it up. Divide students into six groups and give each a different task. Depending on your town, you may want to leave out one task or several and you may like to assign larger numbers of students to some tasks than others (e.g. if your town has plenty of trips and scenic outings but very little nightlife).

2. Assign a time each week, or set the project for homework over a number of weeks when students have access to a video camera to carry out the task. Depending on the equipment you have available, groups may have to do this on a rota basis.

3. Each group is responsible for editing their own film.

4. When they are all finished, you can get students to upload the films to a wiki or a ning. These can then be viewed by incoming students as an introduction to the town.

Variations

- Other topics for similar projects could involve: sport and games, clubs and societies, voluntary organisations, areas of the town/local communities. All of these can be constructed in a similar way and will get students actively involved in finding out more about the L2 community and talking to people.

- If you are not teaching in the L2 country, it will still be possible to do this activity if you find interviewees among L2 speakers you know, or people for whom the L2 will be a lingua franca with your students.

Worksheet 1 Task sheet

1. *Cafés, pubs and restaurants*

Your group's task is to make a 5-minute introduction to good cafés, pubs and restaurants. Film the outside and inside (if you can get permission). Say why you recommend the places. Include at least one short interview with a café owner or a satisfied customer!

2. *Shopping*

Your group's task is to make a 5-minute introduction to good shopping areas and your favourite shops. Film the outside and inside (if you can get permission). Say why you recommend the places. Include at least one short interview with a shop owner or shoppers who can tell you where they like shopping!

3. *Walks, places to picnic*

Your group's task is to make a 5-minute introduction to some interesting or pretty walks in the area. Film the walks. Say why you recommend them. Include at least one short interview with someone from the area!

4. *Cinemas, other entertainment*

Your group's task is to make a 5-minute introduction to cinemas, theatres, concert venues, etc. Film the outside and inside (if you can get permission). Say what kind of entertainment is offered in each place. Include at least one short interview with someone who works there or people who are leaving after seeing a film, play or concert!

5. *Nightlife*

Your group's task is to make a 5-minute introduction to nightlife – clubs and bars. Film the outside and inside (if you can get permission). Say why you recommend the places. Include at least one short interview with someone who works there or with a customer!

6. *Trips and outings*

Your group's task is to make a 5-minute introduction to trips and outings. Film as many places as possible, or, if you cannot, film pictures from brochures. Say why you recommend the places. Include at least one short interview with a tour operator or with a satisfied customer!

Activity 85: Interviews: What do you think of . . . ?

Aim:	To make a short video on people's views of the town where students are studying
Level:	Pre-intermediate up
Time:	Requires project time allocation over a number of weeks, or could be set as homework
Materials:	Video camera(s), task sheet
Preparation:	Type up the task sheet students prepare and make copies of it

Language practice	
Functions	giving opinions and preferences
Skills	listening, speaking
Language areas	as required

Procedure

1. Tell students they have to interview you about the town you are living/ teaching in. Brainstorm a list of topics on the board.

2. Ask them to work in pairs to make up questions on the topics. Collect these in.

3. Type up the list for the next lesson, correcting errors and avoiding duplication. Add questions if there seem to be obvious gaps. Make a copy for each pair of students and cut up one copy so there is one question for each pair of students.

4. The next day give each pair of students one question each to ask. Let them interview you.

5. Give out the complete list of questions to the pairs of students. Ask them to choose five or six questions from the list as 'their' questions.

6. Tell them that they are going to work in pairs to interview three people using the questions they have chosen.

7. Assign a time each week, or set the project for homework over a number of weeks when the students can have access to a video camera to carry

out the task. Depending on the equipment you have available, groups may have to do this on a rota basis.

8. Each group is responsible for editing their own film.

9. When they are all finished you can get students to upload the films to a wiki or a ning. They can view each other's interviews.

Variation

Other topics for similar interviews could involve such general topics as work, leisure time, holidays. it is probably best to avoid very controversial topics. All of these can be set up in a similar way and will get students actively involved in finding out more about the L2 community and talking to people.

Activity 86: Community Placements

Aim: To get students to join the L2 community and to keep a reflective log

Level: Pre-intermediate up

Time: Requires project time allocation over a number of weeks, or could be set as homework

Materials: None

Preparation: You will need to compile a list of organisations in your town that students could join

Language practice	
Functions	as required
Skills	listening, speaking, writing, reading
Language areas	as required

Procedure

1. Compile a list of organisations in your town that students can join. These could include working for voluntary organisations such as charity shops, the Citizens' Advice Bureau, volunteers in hospitals and nursing homes, conservation groups, clubs and social groups, church groups, etc. (In practice, we have always found the volunteer groups and charity workers to be the most welcoming to foreign students, though, for students who are Christian, church groups have also provided a warm welcome, and for sports enthusiasts clubs and teams have been a good entry point into the community. Many of our students have really enjoyed working in charity shops or visiting old peoples' homes.)

2. Give the list to the students and tell them that their homework for this week is to join one of these organisations (if they are not already doing something similar in their spare time). They should pick something they would enjoy doing or learning about and make an arrangement to go once a week for at least an hour. They should keep a reflective log of their experiences, detailing conversations they have had and describing what they have learnt about the L2 culture and community.

3. Set the project for homework over a number of weeks. It may help if you make this assignment assessed!

4. Students can give short presentations of their logs at the end of term, or, if you prefer, you can get students to keep blogs where they can interact and comment on each other's entries, or interact through Facebook, a wiki or a ning, where they can also post photos.

Note: If you are not teaching in the L2 country, it may still be possible to do this activity if you can access L2 expatriate communities via cultural organisations, such as the Alliance Française, Goethe Institut or British Council.

Activity 87: International E-pals

Aim: To get students to communicate with an e-pal in the L2 over a period of time

Level: Pre-intermediate up

Time: Requires project time allocation over a number of weeks, or could be set as homework

Materials: None

Preparation: You will need to investigate a number of sites for linking penpals

Language practice	
Functions	as required
Skills	listening, speaking, writing, reading
Language areas	as required

Procedure

1. Set up an online social network for your students: find an e-pal site or chat group for them to join, depending on their interests. If you have contacts with a partner school or college in another country you can set up a Facebook page for them to network. If you do not have contacts in the L2 country, there are a number of e-pal sites, which cater for schools and colleges. You should be mindful of net safety when setting up online contacts for students. The British Council has a list of a number of sites designed for schools and colleges: www.britishcouncil.org/learning-ie-school-partnerships.htm

2. If you have a computer lab you could give them a regular slot to network, otherwise set a homework slot. If they are at early stages of language learning, you could specify simple topics for them to write about, linked to your syllabus, e.g. 'My family', 'What I like doing', etc.

Activity 88: Guest Speakers

Aim: To give students the opportunity of listening to and interact-
               ing with a variety of L2 speakers

Level: Intermediate up

Time: Requires time allocation over a number of weeks

Materials: None

Preparation: You will need to investigate possibilities for guest speakers

Language practice	
Functions	as required
Skills	listening, speaking
Language areas	as required

Procedure

1. Compile a list of speakers you could invite into your classroom to give short talks on various topics. You may like to organise this around topics the students are interested in or around your syllabus topics. If you are not in the L2-speaking country, you may still be able to find speakers from cultural organisations, among the expatriate community, or from among your friends and colleagues. If this is not possible, invite in virtual speakers – some references for podcasts and YouTube videos are given below.

2. Before the speaker comes, tell students briefly what they will speak about and get them to prepare some questions they would like to ask. Get one student to be responsible for thanking the speaker.

3. On the day, organise the session so that there is time for questions after the talk.

Virtual speakers

Here are some suggestions for 'virtual guest speakers'. The Internet contains many sites where presentations are video recorded and your students might be more than happy to explore these and select some likely candidates.

- Naomi Wolf on The End of America – how democracies close down: www. youtube.com/watch?v=RjALf12PAWc

- The Story of Stuff: entertaining and accessible talk on the environment: www.youtube.com/watch?v=gLBE5QAYXp8

- A sociology professor talks about the changing nature of family life in the US: www.youtube.com/watch?v=F0Oqeov0Gcw

- National Geographic talk on whether time travel is actually possible! www. youtube.com/watch?v=SafwXdP7ylc&feature=fvw

- Lonely Planet talks about various countries: www.youtube.com/ watch?v=6HDoRchR6Sg   www.youtube.com/watch?v=UXT6TJ6vKLo www.youtube.com/watch?v=PJFPqOkNsio   www.youtube.com/watch? v=yQa_cGF-YGQ

- Talk on the different phases of culture shock: www.youtube.com/watch? v=tPfB6GIjM9Qfmt=18&annotation_id=annotation_80947&feature=iv www.youtube.com/watch?v=H82IFq0HbTQ&feature=related

Activity 89: Chat Corner

Aim: To provide students with conversational opportunities with L2 speakers

Level: Elementary up

Time: In students' free time

Materials: A congenial place to meet (e.g. student lounge)

Preparation: Research sources of potential 'chatters' (see Point 1 below); advertise and if necessary establish funding arrangement with school

Language practice	
Functions	as required
Skills	listening, speaking
Language areas	as required

Procedure

1. Research sources of potential 'chatters' – people who are willing to spend an hour or so a week chatting to students. These could include, for example, university and college students or retired people. Arrange advertising posters in places where you might attract 'chatters'. Some people may be very willing to do this for free; for example university or college students who are learning the students' L1 might be interested in a 'language exchange' corner. If necessary, see if you could establish a funding arrangement with school to pay students or college students (at the Université de Bordeaux we did this and it worked very well).

2. Establish a 'chat corner' – a congenial place to sit and talk (e.g. student lounge) and find the best times to set up official 'chat corner' slots (e.g. lunch hours or after class, etc.).

3. Draw up a rota. Try to have more than one chatter 'on duty' at a time.

Simulations: let's pretend

Initial note: The activities in this section are whole-class simulations: role-plays where the classroom becomes a simulated environment (an airport, a restaurant, a town centre) and the students become characters in that environment (a plane passenger, a waiter, a lost tourist). The simulations in this section focus on everyday situations involving transactions of goods and services: tourist information, shops, hotels, restaurants, etc. They have a game-like element with a goal to be accomplished: this fixed outcome is satisfying for the students and the game-like feel is relaxing and non-threatening.

The tasks have been written so that they can be done on two levels, according to the language level of the students and how familiar and comfortable they feel with roleplay. For a low-level class, or one that is unused to roleplay, the simulation involves a simple transaction: asking for or offering services. For a higher-level class, or one that is used to roleplay, there is a second set of role cards that can be given out in addition to the simple cards. These cards add another dimension to the first set: for example, in the hotel simulation, a simple roleplay card states: *You want a room for two with a shower and a sea view.* Cards that can be added to this are:

- *You have had a long journey and feel grumpy and tired.*
- *You are fussy: it is worth trying different hotels to get what you want.*
- *Offer a large tip if they find you a room.*

Activity 90: A Bed for the Night

Aim: To practise enquiring about and booking a hotel room

Level: Elementary upwards

Time: 40 minutes

Materials: Role cards worksheet

Preparation: Copy enough tourist cards for approximately two thirds of your class; copy the corresponding hotel room cards

Language practice	
Functions	likes and preferences
Skills	reading, speaking
Language areas	present continuous, would like to, want, have got

Procedure

1. Organise the class into a 'town', 'street' or 'square' – that is, move desks either into two rows with a space in the middle (street) or into a square with space in the middle (town square).

2. Designate four desks as hotels. The hotels should have as much space between them as possible. Put a number of chairs behind each hotel. Place a name card on each hotel.

3. Ask approximately a third of your students to be 'receptionists'. Divide them evenly between the hotels and ask them to stand or sit at their hotel desks. Give them the hotel room cards, dividing them evenly between the hotels.

4. The rest of your students are tourists. Give out the tourist cards.

5. The tourists should go from hotel to hotel asking for a room until they find one which suits their requirements. When they have found their hotel they should 'go in', that is, sit down at one of the chairs in their hotel area. You will be able to see when the game is finished because everyone will be sitting down.

Variations

1. You can add a competitive element by giving out fewer hotel room cards than tourist cards and ask the tourists to find a room that is as near as possible to what they want, but be prepared to compromise.

2. You can also add a competitive element by giving out more hotel room cards than tourist cards. The receptionists should now try to persuade customers to take their rooms. The customers should hold out for what they are looking for and try to persuade receptionists to offer a price reduction.

3. You can give out the additional role cards to customers and tourists.

Worksheet 1 Role cards

Tourist cards

You want a twin-bedded room with a shower and a sea view for 2 nights.

You want a double room with a shower and a sea view for 2 nights.

You want a single room with a shower and a sea view for 2 nights.

You want a family room with a shower and a sea view for 2 nights.

You want a twin-bedded room with a bath for 3 nights.

You want a double room with a bath for 3 nights.

You want a single room with a bath for 3 nights.

You want a family room with a bath for 3 nights.

Photocopying of this worksheet is permitted: enlarge as necessary
© Jill Hadfield and Zoltán Dörnyei 2013

Hotel room cards

Available: Room 101, 1 twin-bedded room with a shower and a sea view for 2 nights: £90 pn

Available: Room 208, 1 double room with a shower and a sea view for 2 nights: £90 pn

Available: Room 206, 1 single room with a shower and a sea view for 2 nights: £70 pn

Available: Room 407, 1 family room with a shower and a sea view for 2 nights: £110 pn

Available: Room 104, 1 twin-bedded room with a bath for 3 nights: £70 pn

Available: Room 508, 1 double room with a bath for 3 nights: £70 pn

Available: Room 306, 1 single room with a bath for 3 nights: £50 pn

Available: Room 407, 1 family room with a bath for 3 nights: £85 pn

Worksheet 2 Additional role cards

Tourist

You have had a long journey and are feeling tired and grumpy.

You are very fussy. Make a lot of enquiries about the room. You don't want to be near the bar or restaurant. You don't like being too high up. It's worth trying different hotels to get what you want.

You are sure you booked a room in this hotel. Have they lost your reservation?

You will take anything. You just need to go to sleep!

You don't want to spend too much money. Go to different hotels to see where you can get the best bargain. Offer a large tip to get what you want.

Receptionist

You are keen to sell your rooms. Be prepared to bargain.

Tell customers that hotels in the town are booked up. Try to get them to change to one of the rooms you have.

You're tired and want to go home. Try to get everything sorted out as quickly as possible.

You enjoy chatting to customers and finding out about them.

Activity 91: Doing the Shopping

Aim:	To practise shopping in the L2 culture
Level:	Elementary up
Time:	20–30 minutes
Materials:	Various role cards
Preparation:	Copy enough shopping lists for approximately two thirds of your class; copy the corresponding goods cards

Language practice	
Functions	asking for goods
Skills	listening, speaking
Language areas	I'd like. Have you got? How much does it cost?

Procedure

1. Organise the class into a 'town', 'street' or 'square' – that is, move desks either into two rows with a space in the middle (street) or into a square with space in the middle (town square).

2. Designate four desks as shops. The shops should have as much space between them as possible. Place a name card on each shop: Butcher, Chemist, etc. Ask approximately a third of your students to be 'shop-keepers'. Divide them evenly between the shops and ask them to stand or sit at their 'counters'. Give them the goods cards that are appropriate for their shop. Ask them to make up prices for their goods and to write them by the items.

3. The rest of your students are shoppers. Give out the shopping lists.

4. The tourists should go from shop to shop to find the goods on their list. When they obtain an item they can cross it off their list. When they have found their goods, they should sit down. You will be able to see when the game is finished because everyone will be sitting down.

Variations

1. Give the shoppers an additional list. This time, tell the shopkeepers to cross an item off their list when they 'sell' it. The aim is for the shoppers to obtain as many of the items on their lists as possible.

2. Give all shopkeepers all four lists. They are rival supermarkets. Each should write prices by their goods. Tell the shoppers they really want to save money! They must 'shop around' to find the best price for their items.

3. Give additional role cards to shoppers and shopkeepers.

- 1 kg tomatoes
- 2 steaks
- 500 g cheese
- shampoo

- 1 kg bananas
- toothpaste
- flour
- 1 kg chicken pieces

- 1 lettuce
- 500 g mince
- 6 eggs
- soap

- 1 kg apples
- 1 chicken
- 1 litre milk
- film

- cauliflower
- 6 lamb chops
- 1 bag rice
- aspirin

- 5 kg potatoes
- 1 kg sausages
- bag of pasta
- vitamin pills

- 6 oranges
- leg of lamb
- olive oil
- plasters

- 1 kg carrots
- joint of beef
- olive oil
- plasters

GROCER	FRUIT SHOP	CHEMIST	BUTCHER
• cheese	• tomatoes	• shampoo	• steak
• flour	• bananas	• toothpaste	• chicken
• eggs	• lettuce	• soap	• chicken pieces
• milk	• apples	• aspirin	• mince
• rice	• cauliflower	• vitamin pills	• lamb chops
• pasta	• oranges	• plasters	• sausages
• olive oil	• potatoes	• face cream	• leg of lamb
• coffee	• carrots	• film	• joints of beef

Worksheet 3 Additional role cards

Shoppers

You are very chatty. Talk to as many shopkeepers and people in the queue as possible.

You are very picky. Complain about the quality of the things you are buying.

You cannot understand why everything is so expensive. Complain loudly!

You are short of time and want to get your shopping done as quickly as possible.

Shopkeepers

You want to know in detail what kind of goods the shopper wants, for example:

- steaks: how big?
- aspirin: soluble/non-soluble? How many in a packet?
- coffee: ground or beans, dark or light roast, decaffeinated?
- apples: green or red, small or large? etc.

You particularly dislike customers who take up time by chatting.

You enjoy your job and like chatting to customers. Take time to get to know them!

Try to get the shoppers to buy something else as well as the item on their list. Be persuasive!

Activity 92: Where Can I Get a Cup of Coffee?

Aim: To practise asking for directions and information

Level: Elementary up

Time: 20–30 minutes

Materials: Role cards, maps

Preparation: Copy enough blank maps and tourist role cards for approximately two thirds of your class; copy the additional role cards if you want to play the advanced version; copy the marked maps for approximately one third of your class; copy the residents' cards for this third if you want to play the advanced version

Language practice

Functions	asking for and giving directions
Skills	listening and speaking
Language areas	Where is . . . ? How do I get to? Turn left/right, take the . . . on the left/right

Procedure

1. Organise the class into a 'town', 'street' or 'square', that is, move desks either into two rows with a space in the middle (street) or into a square with space in the middle (town square).

2. Give out blank maps to two thirds of the class. Tell them they are tourists and do not know where anything is. Give them each a role card.

3. Give the marked maps to the rest of the class and tell them they are residents.

4. Tell all the class to begin at High Street at the place marked 'You are here'. The tourists should find where the places are on the map by asking directions from the residents. As the game progresses they will also be able to find directions from other tourists.

5. As they find directions they should draw their route and mark the place on the map. They should then ask directions for the next place from that place.

6. When they have found all the places, they should sit down and tell the person sitting next to them about their 'day out'. You will be able to see when the game is finished because everyone will be sitting down.

Variation

1. Put residents in pairs and give out the maps and additional role cards. Allow them a little time to think up some interesting 'facts' about their town and decide what is worth seeing and what isn't, which restaurants are good, etc.

2. While they are doing this, give out the tourist maps, role cards and additional role cards to the tourists. Ask them to think of reasons why they have chosen to do these things.

3. Then put tourists with different role cards in pairs. Start the roleplay.

Worksheet 1 Town maps

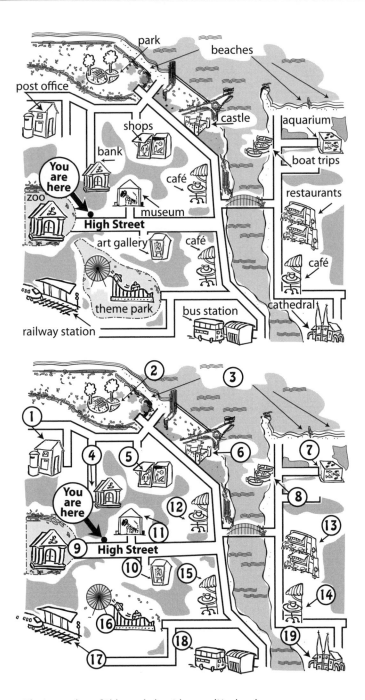

Worksheet 2 Role cards

You have a day in Seacastle. You want to:

- go to the museum
- change some money
- have a coffee and a sandwich
- go to a nice beach
- go out for dinner

You have a day in Seacastle. You want to:

- go to the art gallery
- buy some stamps
- have a picnic in the park
- go shopping
- go out for dinner

You have a day in Seacastle. You want to:

- go to the castle
- have a picnic on the beach
- go shopping
- go out for dinner

You have a day in Seacastle. You want to:

- go to the cathedral
- go out for lunch
- go on a boat trip
- catch the train to London

You have a day in Seacastle. You want to:

- go to the aquarium
- go out for lunch
- go to a concert in the park
- catch the bus to the airport

You have a day in Seacastle. You want to:

- go to the zoo
- have a picnic on the beach
- go to the theme park
- go out for dinner

Worksheet 3 Additional role cards

Residents

You have lived in Seacastle for years and know it very well. You have strong opinions about what is worth doing in the town and what is not worth doing. You love talking about your town and telling tourists interesting facts and giving your opinions.

Tourists

You have good reasons for wanting to do certain things on your day in Seacastle. Your friend has other ideas. Be prepared to argue – but also to take advice from people who know the town well.

Activity 93: What's On?

Aim: To practise enquiring about and booking entertainment

Level: Elementary up

Time: 20–30 minutes

Materials: Entertainment cards, tickets

Preparation: Make one copy of the entertainment cards; make labels for the theatre, cinema, etc.; make a number of small pieces of paper for each place to act as tickets; you will need as many tickets for each place as there are students in your class

Language practice	
Functions	asking about entertainment, requests
Skills	listening and speaking
Language areas	What's on tonight? I'd like . . . , Have you got . . . ?

Procedure

1. Organise the class into a 'town', 'street' or 'square'; that is, move desks either into two rows with a space in the middle (street) or into a square with space in the middle (town square).

2. Designate six desks as the Theatre, Cinema, Concert Hall, Opera House, Stadium and Festival Office. Give each a label.

3. Ask six students to sit at the 'ticket offices'.

4. The rest of your students are tourists. Group them in pairs and tell them they are wandering down the main street in the city and decide to have a night out. They should call in at each place and see what's on, then decide what to do together and go back to book the tickets.

5. When they have obtained their tickets they should sit down. They can discuss their choices with the pair next to them. You will be able to see when the game is finished because everyone will be sitting down.

Variation

Make a smaller number of tickets for each place. Some places will then get booked out early and the pairs of tourists will have to make alternative choices. You can make the game more difficult by only giving out the same total number of tickets as the number of 'tourists'.

Worksheet 1 Ticket cards

Theatre

Tonight:

Main Hall:
Phantom of the opera (musical)
(7.30 p.m.)

Tickets at £30,
£25, £20, £18

Little Theatre:
Sally and me (a hilarious comedy about female friendships)
(8.00 p.m.)

Tickets £20, £18,
£15, £10

Cinema

Screen 1: Golden Oldies: *Jaws*
(5.15 p.m.)

Screen 2: *The language teacher* (horror; 6.30 and 9.15 p.m.)

Screen 3: *Autumn Leaves* (romantic comedy; 6 and 8 p.m.)

Screen 4:
Spiderweb (chilling spy thriller; 5.30 and 7.30 p.m.)

Tickets: £4

Festival Office

Jazz Festival:
Music live in pubs and parks from 6 p.m.

Pubs: The King's Arms, The Edinburgh Castle, The Wild Goose

Parks: Central Park, Albert Park

Combined ticket to all venues: £10

Concert Hall

The Berlin Philharmonic:
a programme of Mozart and Haydn (8 p.m.)

Tickets £15, £12,
£10

Opera House

5 p.m.: *Swan lake* (ballet)

8 p.m.: Bizet's *Carmen*

Tickets: £40, £35,
£30, £20

Stadium

6. 30 p.m.: Rugby – Wallabies vs. Springboks

Activity 94: Airport

Aim: To practise asking for and giving information

Level: Elementary up

Time: 20–30 minutes

Materials: Rolecards, tokens

Preparation: Copy enough passenger cards for approximately two thirds of your class; make one copy of the help desk, transport desk, tourist information and flight information cards; you will also need a supply of tokens: counters or small pieces of card for each desk. Make copies of the additional role cards if you want to play the advanced version

Language practice

Functions	asking for and giving information
Skills	listening and speaking
Language areas	Where is . . . ? How do I get to . . . ? What time . . . ? How can I . . . ?

Procedure

1. Organise the classroom into an 'airport' with a large central space and the four information desks in different areas. Label each desk.

2. Ask one third of your students to be the information officers. Divide them as evenly as possible between the four desks and give them the relevant information cards.

3. Ask the remaining students to be the passengers. Give each a passenger card.

4. Ask students to imagine they are in an airport and have a number of questions. They should go to the appropriate desk to ask for information. When they get the information they require they should collect a token from the desk. When they have four different tokens they can sit down.

5. The game is finished when all passengers have their tokens and are sitting down.

Variation

Give out additional cards to information officers and passengers.

Worksheet 1 Passenger cards

- Your suitcase did not arrive at baggage reclaim. It is dark blue with a red strap.
- You want to book a hotel: a comfortable one near the city centre.
- You want to know where to get transport to the hotel.
- You want to fly on to Rome in three days' time. What time are the flights?

- YOU HAVE LOST YOUR CHILD! – a little girl called Suzette. When you have found her, find out the following things:
- Your flight to Singapore NG 239 is delayed – how long?
- If it is a long time, you want to go to the city centre: ask where to get a taxi.
- Ask what there is to do in town that is suitable for children.

- You have missed your 9 a.m. flight to London – how long till the next one?
- If it is a long time you will go into town. Find out where you can get a bus.
- Ask for a map of the city centre.
- OH NO! YOU'VE LOST YOUR PASSPORT! A New Zealand passport No. 237809.

- You are meeting a friend at the airport who is flying in from a different city. The name is Alex Jordan. Your name is Jo Peters. The problem is: your friend was not at the meeting place.
- When you find your friend, find out about transport to the city.
- Find a cheap hostel, near the centre.
- Book your next flight: to Paris in a week's time.

- You fell over and cut your knee. It might need stitches. Find out where you can see a doctor or nurse. When you have dealt with that, find out some more information:
- You have a connecting flight to Singapore. Find out where to go.
- On your way back in two weeks' time, you want to stay here for two days. Book your hotel now. You want a medium price hotel near the centre.
- Arrange to hire a car for the two days.

- You left your jacket on the plane. Find out where the lost property office is.
- You need to know how to get to the city centre.
- You need a hotel for three days in the city centre.
- You want to know what trips and tours are available.

Worksheet 2 Information cards

Help Desk

- A suitcase has been found: dark blue with a red strap
- A lost child, Suzette, turned up at the medical centre. She doesn't speak English. She is with the nurse there. Tel. extension: 3465
- A New Zealand passport has been handed in: no. 237809
- Medical Centre near Exit B
- Lost Property Office near Check-in Counter 6
- Alex Jordan is waiting for Jo Peters at Exit A

Flight Information

- Flights to Rome daily 10 a.m. and 3 p.m.; check in Counter 12; departs Gate 1
- Flights to Paris daily 11 a.m.; check in Counter 4; departs gate 2
- Flights to Singapore daily except Sunday 1 p.m.; check in counter 5; departs Gate 3
- Flights to London daily 9 a.m. and 5 p.m.; check in Counter 6; departs Gate 4
- Departure tax payable at the bank
- New information in: Flight NG 239 to Singapore delayed 6 hours

Transport Desk

- Buses to the city centre every 10 minutes; journey time 20 minutes: Exit A
- Taxi stand: Exit B
- Rail link: trains to town at half past every hour: Exit C down escalator.
- Hotel buses: Exit D

Car Hire Form

Type of car: _____

Name: _____

Hire period: from _____
to _____

Driver licence no. _____
_____

Credit card no. _____
_____

Signature:

Tourist Information

Hotels

***** Embassy, £150 pn, Castle Street, city centre

**** Star, £100 pn, Museum Street, city centre

*** Castle Inn, £80 pn, Bay Road, city centre

** Railway Inn, £50 pn, Station Road, city centre

* Kangaroo Backpackers' Hostel, Hill Road, city centre, £20 pn, Dormitory £10 pn

Tourist attractions

- City Museum, open 9–5 daily, admission free
- Zoo, open daily 9–6, admission £8 adult, £4 child
- Art gallery, open daily except Mondays, admission £5 adult, £3 child
- Castle, open daily except Tuesdays, admission £7 adult, £4 child

Trips

- City tour, half day £15, whole day £25, depart 9 a.m. and 1 p.m. from all hotels
- Riverboat cruise, 2 hours £20, leaves every hour on the hour from West Quay
- Dinner Cruise, 7 p.m., departure from West Quay, £40 includes dinner
- Kayaking on the river, £10 per hour, kayak hire from West Quay

Worksheet 3 Additional role cards

Information Officers	Passengers

Information Officers

- Your shift is ending soon. You want to deal with queries as quickly as possible and go home.

- You deal with a lot of foreigners. The best way to help them understand is to speak VERY LOUDLY.

- You are very chatty and like to welcome travellers and give them a lot of information.

- You are rather scatterbrained and keep losing information.

Passengers

- Travel makes you very nervous. You like to confirm details several times to make sure.

- You don't hear very well.

- You don't understand English very well. Ask staff to repeat.

- You are in a hurry.

- You like to ask for a lot of extra information – staff are there to help you so you can take as much time as you want.

Activity 95: Taking It Back

Aim:	To give students practice in complaining and returning sub-standard goods in different circumstances
Level:	Intermediate up
Time:	20–30 minutes
Materials:	Role cards, picture cards, shop cards
Preparation:	Copy and cut up a set of role cards, and a set of picture cards; make a set of shop name cards for the six shops (Takeaway, Clothes Shop, Supermarket, Electronics Shop, DVD Rental, Camping and Outdoor Store); you will need to make copies of the money picture and of the Customer and Assistant cards if you want to play the 'advanced' version

Language practice	
Functions	complaining, apologising, giving reasons
Skills	listening and speaking
Language areas	I'm afraid that . . . I'm sorry but . . . past simple, too . . . enough

Procedure

1. Lead-in: bring, if you can, an example of faulty workmanship to the class (e.g. shrunk garment, pan with broken handle, video or DVD that won't play). Explain that you bought it last week and this happened the first time you washed/used/played it. Ask the class what they would do/say. Ask them for any experiences that have had of taking things back and complaining.

2. Arrange the classroom like a street or town square.

3. Put the shop name cards (Takeaway, Clothes Shop, Supermarket, Electronics Shop, DVD Rental, Camping and Outdoor Store) at six desks so the names are clearly visible. Get two students to be assistants in each shop. Give them the picture cards appropriate for their shop.

4. Give complaint cards to the rest of the students.

5. These customers visit the shops and complain about the situation described on the card.

6. The assistants should select the matching 'new object' card and hand it to Student A, making an apology.

Variation

- Copy more of the money picture cards and give them out to the shops.

- Photocopy the Customer and Assistant cards and give these out to the students.

Worksheet 1 Complaint cards

- You have just bought a takeaway pizza. Looking at the bill you can see that they have charged you too much. Complain politely and ask for the money back.
- You bought a T-shirt last week. The first time you washed it it shrank. Take it back to the shop and complain.
- You bought a garden chair last week from the outdoor shop. Today a friend sat on it and it fell apart. Take it back to the shop and complain.

- You rented a DVD yesterday. There is something wrong with it and it won't play.
- You bought some milk yesterday. When you opened it, it was sour.
- You have just bought a takeaway pizza. It is cold!

- You bought an iPod yesterday. When you unpacked it you found the earphones were damaged.
- You bought a tent for your holiday. The holiday was a disaster – the tent pole snapped and the tent leaks!
- You have just bought a takeaway salad. When you started eating you found a spider in your lettuce!

- You bought a skirt yesterday. When you got home you found a small hole in it.
- You bought some orange juice yesterday. When you got home you found it was past its sell-by date.
- You bought a digital camera yesterday. When you tried it out it didn't work.

- You rented a DVD yesterday but when you got home there was nothing in the box!
- You bought a garden umbrella yesterday but when you got home you found it was ripped.
- You bought a shirt last week but when you washed it the colour ran. You wanted a red shirt not a pink one!

- You bought a bottle of olive oil yesterday but when you got home you found it had already been opened.
- You bought a TV but when it was delivered it was damaged.
- You rented a DVD last night but the assistant put the wrong one in the box.

Worksheet 2 Picture cards

Worksheet 3 Role cards

Customer

- You do not want a replacement. You want your money back. Be firm.

- You do not want a replacement. You would prefer your money back – try to negotiate politely.

- You do not really want a replacement. You would really like your money back but realise this may not be possible.

- You are quite angry about what happened and are determined to get your money back.

- You do not want a replacement. You want your money back but you are not very good at arguing . . .

- You do not want a replacement. You know your legal rights.

Assistant

- Your firm's policy is not to give refunds if possible, though they will refund money in special circumstances. Try to negotiate giving a credit note or replacement instead of money.

- Your firm's policy is never to give refunds. Offer a replacement or a credit note.

- Your firm's policy is never to give refunds. Be very firm about this. Suggest that it was the customer's fault.

- Your boss gets very angry if you give refunds to customers. Try to find reasons why you should not refund the money.

Cultural events

Activity 96: Film Screenings

Aim: To give students an opportunity to see and discuss films in the L2

Level: Intermediate up (earlier if shown with subtitles)

Time: Requires a time slot out of class time each week/fortnight/ month

Materials: DVDs, DVD player

Preparation: Make sure your establishment has a licence to show DVDs of movies to groups; establish a regular time slot, draw up a list of movies and make a calendar for distribution

Language practice	
Functions	discussing films
Skills	listening, speaking
Language areas	language for opinions and preferences, language for film

Procedure

- Establish a regular time slot, draw up a list of L2 movies and make a calendar for distribution to students. You can also make film posters for the week the movie is being shown. Make a rota of staff who will be in charge of showing the movie and leading a discussion afterwards. (This need not be onerous – you can organise it so that staff are only on duty once or twice a year – and if you let staff choose movies they want to watch, it need not be a chore!)

- Show the movie. If you have a lower-level group, subtitles will be essential, and even with a higher level group subtitles can be a valuable listening tool. Hold a discussion afterwards.

Activity 97: Foodies

Aim:	To let students experience eating and making food from the L2 culture
Level:	Elementary up
Time:	Requires a one-off slot out of class time at regular intervals, for example each month (or within class time if you want to make a project out of it and your school has a kitchen)
Materials:	Ingredients for the recipes, kitchen and equipment, student cafeteria or classroom for consuming the finished products
Preparation:	Decide on the format of this activity best suited to your class/school; research recipes

Language practice	
Functions	following recipes, discussing food
Skills	listening, speaking, writing
Language areas	imperatives, likes and dislikes, food vocabulary

Procedure

1. Decide on a one-off or regular (e.g. every term, once a month) time slot for a food evening.

2. Decide on the theme: for example, a Tapas Evening, a Sushi Evening, a New Zealand/Australian Barbecue, Chinese Dumplings, French Wine and Cheese, etc.

3. Collect a number of recipes.

4. If you have access to a large kitchen, you can begin the evening with everyone making recipes together. If not, you can allocate recipes to groups of students to prepare at home and bring in. Students can type up and illustrate their recipes and you can copy them to make a recipe booklet for everyone.

5. Enjoy!

Activity 98: Festivals

Aim: To give students an opportunity to experience L2 festivals

Level: Elementary up

Time: Requires an (irregular) time slot to coincide with festival

Materials: Depending on festival – videos, reading, other materials for festival

Preparation: Depending on festival

Language practice	
Functions	talking about customs and festivals
Skills	listening, speaking, writing, reading
Language areas	present simple, imperatives

Procedure

1. Research dates of festivals and plan some class time into your syllabus.

2. Decide on the format of the session:
   - you may use reading material or videos as background information
   - you may want to plan in a 'Listen and Do' or 'Listen and Make' activity such as making a Mexican piñata, Chinese lanterns or Easter cards (particularly important with younger learners)
   - if you are teaching in the L2 culture, you may be able to schedule a class outing to experience the festival first hand
   - if you are not teaching in the L2 culture, you may want to plan in a school event to re-create the festival (e.g. Easter egg hunt, Thai water splashing festival, etc.).

3. Even if your main focus is experiencing the festival, you might schedule a background information session first where students do a Webquest or jigsaw reading activity to find and share information, or watch and discuss a video. Below are some web addresses with YouTube videos of festivals.

YouTube addresses for festivals

- LaTomatina Spain: www.youtube.com/watch?v=JzWWhqL0ruY

- San Fermin: www.youtube.com/watch?v=f7DgX9rcJFE

- Fallas Valencia: www.youtube.com/watch?v=Q4MWJvJTefY

- Festival of lights France: www.youtube.com/watch?v=6_cLwKrzgosfeature=related

- Mid-Autumn moon festival: www.youtube.com/watch?v=CaFBLgaM3d4–feature=related

- Lion dance: www.youtube.com/watch?v=pxm0hEVF2Egfeature=related

- Tanabata Japan: www.youtube.com/watch?v=a_hBPTDD9to

- Powhiri Maori: www.youtube.com/watch?v=1qRRtuZZB-M

- Oktoberfest: www.youtube.com/watch?v=i3Xag0wPcHA

- Italy (also WebvisionItaly.com): www.youtube.com/watch?v=utLhe0l7yhw

- A British Christmas: www.youtube.com/watch?v=taVWVLK1wEc

- Thanksgiving: www.youtube.com/watch?v=5133moUGDgQ

- Easter egg hunt: www.youtube.com/watch?v=4JW_eG3b_N8

- White House Easter egg roll: www.youtube.com/watch?v=p--lkfu2_7k&NR=1

- Obby oss: www.youtube.com/watch?v=tDcmj3QU0dc

- Guy Fawkes Night: www.youtube.com/watch?v=UKLfR6fU9ew&feature=related

Activity 99: Culture Board

Aim:	To give students information and pictures about various L2 customs
Level:	Elementary up
Time:	Time out of class for reading and contributing to board
Materials:	Pin board, reading material, photos
Preparation:	Put up a pinboard in the classroom; collect reading material and photos of customs and culture of the L2

Language practice	
Functions	describing and discussing culture and customs
Skills	writing, reading
Language areas	as required

Procedure

1. Put up a large pinboard in the classroom. Divide it into areas with ribbon. Label the areas (according to which customs you are focusing on). Have one area labelled 'Comments'.

2. Collect some reading texts and photos on a particular area (e.g. explaining greeting customs) and put these upon the board.

3. Encourage students to read the board and to contribute comments, for example about customs they have found out about, things which surprised them, things they like . . .

4. Change the display regularly.

Part III

From application to implementation

Towards a motivational programme

A comprehensive motivational programme would cover the three main vision-ary areas outlined in Part II of this book: 'Imaging identity' (Chapter 1), 'Mapping the journey' (Chapter 2) and 'Keeping the vision alive' (Chapter 3). We would suggest a short 'induction' module to raise the students' awareness in the first week of a new course, based mainly on the activities in 'Imaging identity' followed by two ongoing parallel processes that involve (a) weekly goal-setting and strategy-mapping activities based on the material in 'Mapping the journey' and (b) weekly identity activities based on the material in 'Keeping the vision alive'. These specific motivational tasks focusing on the learners' future vision would take place within the framework of the course as a whole, alongside and integrated with other more traditional language-learning activities. The third pillar of the L2 Motivational Self System, the enjoyment of the learning experience, would be provided by the whole course through a variety of means such as engaging activities and teacher enthusiasm as well as productive group dynamics leading to a cohesive learner group with appropriate goals and group norms.

Induction module

This module is suitable for the first day or week of a course. Its aim is to work through the processes in 'Imaging identity' in order to create a rich and yet realistic vision of the future L2 self. Within each section in the chapter, activities can be divided up into those suitable for a lead-in or introduction, core activities and follow-up activities. The table below shows how the specific activities fit into this division.

	Introductory activities	Core activities	Follow-up activities
Creating the vision	1, 2, 4, 5	3, 6, 7	8
Substantiating the vision	9	10, 11 (if 3 or 6 are chosen above), 13 (if 7 is chosen above)	12, 14
Counterbalancing the vision	15	16, 17, 18, 19, 20	21
Unifying the vision	22, 23, 24	25, 26, 27	28, 29
Enhancing the vision	30	31, 32	33
From vision to goals	38	34, 35, 36, 37	

We will look at how to organise these activities into each of these alternatives:

- a 'full' programme
- a time-constrained programme
- a language-focused module
- an 'identity project'

A 'full' programme

A 'full' programme would include at least one core activity from each of the five sections of 'Imaging identity'. The activities in 'From vision to goals' could be done after that or following on from 'Substantiating the vision', since they are based on work done in that section. This could be done during the first morning of a language course or taking about forty minutes each morning in the first week of an intensive course.

A time-constrained programme

If you are doing a programme with time constraints (e.g. an evening class) you could choose in the first class to do a visualisation activity – for example,

Activity 6: My Future L2 Self – from 'Creating the vision', followed by some work on *Substantiating the Vision* – for example, Activities 10 or 11 – followed by some definition of long-term goals using Activities 34–37 from 'From vision to goals'.

Language work

It is possible to select activities on the basis of the language students practise to form a combined language-plus-motivation programme. This could be structured via a PPP (Presentation → Practice → Production) approach, where language is introduced and practised in a controlled way, with the motivation activities then forming the free practice activities, or in a task-based format, where the motivation activities constitute the actual tasks, which can then be followed up with Focus on Form activities.

- Activities in 'Creating the vision' typically focus on the present simple/ present continuous tenses and on description and narrative.

- Activities in 'Substantiating the vision' and 'From vision to goals' typically focus on modals (can, will/won't be able to, would like to) and on wishes, predictions and opinions.

- Activities in 'Counterbalancing the vision' and 'Unifying the vision' typically focus on modals (should, ought to, have to, might, need to) and on advice and suggestions.

- Activities in 'Enhancing the vision' focus on present and past tenses (present simple, past simple, present perfect) and on narration and description.

Identity projects

An identity project is, like any other project, a series of activities culminating in a 'product'. In this case, the 'product' is the expression of the learner's L2 identity in some tangible form (e.g. a poster, a display, a fairytale book). In the same way as any other project work, it is organised in a task-based learning format that includes a series of tasks and follow-up language work deriving from the tasks and is based on perceived student needs. The table presents a possible framework for an identity project.

	Product	Language focus
Creating the vision	identity tree posters (Activity 7) or visualisation and mask making (Activities 6 and 8)	• present simple, present continuous, simple past, present perfect • description of appearance, personality, feelings • narrating past experiences
Substantiating the vision	poster creation and display: either Activity 9 or 10 (following on from Activity 6) or Activity 13 (following on from Activity 7)	• present simple, present continuous, simple past, present perfect • description of appearance, personality, feelings • narrating past experiences
Counterbalancing the vision	filmshots, leading to the production of short video clips (Activity 19)	• modals: should, ought to, need to • advice and suggestions
Unifying the vision	song (Activities 23 and 24)	• imperatives, should, ought to • advice and instructions
Enhancing the vision	photo album, poem display, fairytale book (Activities 30, 31, 32 or 33)	• present and past tenses: present simple, past simple, present perfect • narration and description

Mapping the journey

This module follows on from the work in the induction module on substantiating the vision and setting long-term goals. It has three weekly strands:

• establishing short-term goals for the week, breaking these down into precise tasks and organising them into study plans

• learning about and trying out a range of achievement and avoidance strategies for study

• making learning contracts and affirming progress.

Establishing short-term goals, identifying tasks and drawing up study plans

Students will have agreed on long-term class goals and personal goals for the course in the Induction module using Activities 34–38. The subsequent activities (Activities 39–41) are designed to break these long-term goals down into short-term aims and establish weekly goals, while Activities 42–46 are concerned with breaking these weekly goals down further into a series of tasks and then organising the tasks into a study plan.

- *Establishing weekly goals:* Activities 39–41 are designed to form a short sequence that can be used at the beginning of every week to define the week's goals. If time is limited, Activity 40 (Goal Breakdown) could be done on its own and adapted so that part of it is done over the weekend as a homework task. Use this as a basis for a short class discussion on the Monday morning, culminating in either the personal goal statements or the goal wheel display (Activity 41).

- *Identifying tasks:* This identification of weekly goals can then be followed by Activity 42 (Task List), which establishes a list of general tasks for the week, and any of Activities 43–45, which break those general tasks down into more precise ones. A range of activities has been given so that you can vary the format from week to week.

- *Study plans:* Any of the ideas suggested in Activity 46 can be used to help students organise their study time. These can be set for homework on the Monday night if time is short, then either collected in and displayed or signed by you.

Strategies

These can be introduced at the beginning of the course in a 'Strategies Fair', or programmed in on a weekly basis in a 'Strategy Slot'. Activities 47 and 48 are general introductions to the topic, designed to heighten awareness and generate discussion around different working styles and study habits. Thereafter Activities 49–51 introduce the students to a range of achievement strategies: study techniques that can be used across a range of tasks to improve learning, for example by aiding memorisation or improving note-making techniques.

The second half of the cluster of activities focusing on strategies contains avoidance strategies: techniques that can be used to overcome barriers to learning, for example by avoiding distraction or managing time better.

Activities 52–58 introduce a range of techniques in this vein, and Activity 59 offers ways of reviewing and summarising strategies that the students have explored.

Making contracts and affirming progress

This entails making learning intentions public in the form of a 'contract' and in affirming progress. The first activity in this section, Activity 60, is an introductory activity aimed at exploring ways in which students can help each other and ways in which they can team up as 'study buddies'. Thereafter, Activity 61 contains contracts that can be used following identification of short-term goals and weekly study plans at the start of the week, while Activity 62 invites students to assess their own and each other's progress at the end of the week. Activities 63, 64 and 65 are alternative tasks aimed at charting progress and can be used at the end of each week during the course. An example of a weekly schedule for 'Mapping the journey' might look like this:

Time	Aim	Possible activities
Friday afternoon	• Set broad goal for the next week	• Activity 39: Base Camps
Weekend homework	• Break general goal into sub-goals • Identify class aims and personal aims	• Activity 40: Goal Breakdown
Monday morning	• Discussion of personal/class goals • Break goals down into tasks	• Activity 41: Goal Wheels • Activities 42–45
Homework	• Write a study plan • Make a study contract	• Activity 46: Study Plan • Activities 60–61
Midweek	• Introduce a 'strategy of the week'	• Activities 47–51 • Activities 52–58
Friday afternoon	• Self-evaluation and progress recording	• Activities 62–65

Although this programme might take a little time to set up at the beginning of the course, after a couple of weeks the routines you set up should become automatic and more can be done autonomously by the students.

Keeping the vision alive

The aim of the activities in 'Keeping the vision alive' is to extend the vision and to deepen the sense of an L2 identity. The activities here are designed to be used in parallel with the goal-setting activities in 'Mapping the journey', to appeal to the affective as well as the cognitive side of language learning and to keep the learner in touch with the initial vision. There are two strands to 'Keeping the vision alive':

- *Developing identity,* where the aim is to keep in touch with the vision, to develop it in more detail and make sure that it is not lost in the day-to-day business of attending to the learning of various aspects of the language such as doing grammar exercises or writing essays.

- *Making it real,* which provides activities that allow for the use of the L2 in real-life, virtual or simulated, situations, sending the students into the L2 community, or bringing the L2 world into the classroom to make the language and culture come alive for the students.

There are at least four different approaches to integrating the activities into the curriculum:

1. *As part of normal language work:* The simulations (Activities 90–96) and the targeted visualisations (Activities 72–75) can be used as part of normal language work whenever your teaching point lends itself to practice through simulation, with the visualisations being used as short prefaces to prepare students for the simulations.

2. *As term-long projects with a regular weekly time slot and autonomous out-of-class work:* Any one of the activities in 'Identity projects' (Activities 66–71) can be used as a project, culminating in a finished product that can then be displayed, much in the same way as the mini identity project in the 'Induction module' mentioned earlier. Similarly, Activities 84–89 in 'Entering the L2 community' can be set up as projects.

3. *As part of an emerging 'classroom culture':* Certain activities can be done in an ongoing fashion throughout the term, to establish a particular 'culture' in your classroom. They can be sprinkled throughout the term or can occupy a regular 5–10 minute slot. Activities 80–83 in 'Self-belief' are designed to foster an affirming and positive atmosphere and to enhance self-esteem, while the suggestions in 'Entering the L2 community' (Activities 88 and 89) of establishing a chat corner and inviting guest speakers mean establishing a school culture of interaction with the L2 community and L2 speakers.

4. *As occasional 'routine breakers':* Every course needs special occasions and departures from routine! The activities suggested in 'Entering the L2 community', Activity 88 plus Activities 77 and 96–99 are designed to be such special events and to break routine either by inviting guest speakers into the classroom or by organising cultural events.

Enjoyment of the learning experience

In this final section we look at the 'third pillar' of the L2 Motivational Self System: the enjoyment of the learning experience. This section lists a variety of strategies and techniques that the teacher can use to motivate students, in contrast to the procedures described in the previous chapters to help students to find inner motivation through vision. This is obviously a huge area, one which has been treated fully in Zoltán's book on *Motivational strategies in the language classroom* (2001), so we will only give an outline here but provide a selection of useful of further reading at the end.

Any language learning experience consists of a complex relationship between the teacher, the student group, the subject being taught and the learner's sense of self. Enjoyment of the learning experience thus consists of four interrelated areas:

- enjoyment of the teacher's presence and rapport between students and teacher

- enjoyment of the learning group and class climate

- enjoyment of the subject matter and teaching approach

- enjoyment of success and self-esteem.

The absence of any one of these will have a demotivating effect.

In an article based on a survey of language teachers, Dörnyei and Csizér (1998) provided a set of core motivational strategies that teachers could use to create an enjoyable and motivating classroom climate. This list, which they termed the 'Ten commandments for motivating language learners', included the following strategic areas:

1. Set a personal example with your own behaviour.

2. Create a pleasant, relaxed atmosphere in the classroom.

3. Present the tasks properly.

4. Develop a good relationship with the learners.

5. Increase the learner's linguistic self-confidence.

6. Make the language classes interesting.

7. Promote learner autonomy.

8. Personalise the learning process.

9. Increase the learner's goal-orientedness.

10. Familiarise learners with the target language culture.

Of these, 1 and 4 belong to our first category, 'Teacher presence and rapport'; 2 belongs to the second category, 'Group dynamics and class climate'; 3, 6, 8 and 10 to 'Subject matter and teaching approach'; and 5, 7 and 9 to 'Self-esteem and the experience of success'. Let us have a look at some key content areas for each of these rubrics.

1 Teacher presence and rapport

Teacher behaviour

- be pleasant and supportive
- keep a lively pace, energise the students
- have fun and share jokes
- communicate your enthusiasm

Rapport

- have high expectations
- show you care about individual progress
- give individual help and advice
- become aware of student needs and respond to them in your teaching
- make students feel they are accepted for who they are
- listen and respond to student opinions and values
- communicate a personal interest in their lives and interests

2 Group dynamics and class climate

See teacher behaviour and rapport above but also:

- create a pleasant relaxing space, with posters and attractive displays
- establish group norms early on: a set of rules or a contract for group behaviour

- highlight for the students what being in a group involves and do some work on negotiation and compromise skills

- ensure that students do not always work with the same partner or develop cliques: keep relationships fluid

- include personalisation activities, activities that develop empathy and activities that encourage them to find out what they have in common

- round off pair and group work activities with whole class feedback

- work on building a successful 'group legend'

- include activities that lead to tangible collaborative group achievements

- encourage class 'patriotism'

- accentuate the positive

3 Subject matter and teaching approach

Interesting classes

- choose topics that are interesting and relevant to your students' lives

- ensure a student focus

- plan in varied activities and interactions

- select motivating tasks with a clear goal or culminating in a 'product'

- plan in 'routine breakers'

Presenting tasks properly

- make sure aims are clear to the students

- make sure they understand exactly what to do

- engage interest and attention with a lead-in

Personalising the learning process

- provide some individually tailored help, feedback and assignments

- provide materials and tasks with a personal focus to get students to talk about their own lives

Target language culture

- invite guest L2 speakers
- set up 'entering the L2 community' projects
- include a regular 'culture lesson'
- show foreign language films
- set up a chat corner
- celebrate festivals
- hold cultural events

Learner autonomy

- let learners play a part in decisions about curriculum content and class activities
- consult them and take their views into account
- help learners into autonomous learning by providing opportunities for self-study, project work, etc.
- give guidance on strategies for improving self-study abilities

4 **Self-esteem and the experience of success**

Learner goals

- make learners aware of goals
- help them to break goals down and identify tasks
- introduce strategies for attaining goals
- chart progress towards these goals

Self-confidence and self-esteem

- provide a climate of acceptance
- create opportunities for learners to express positive and affirming feelings about each other
- provide learners with regular experience of success

- ensure goals are realistically achievable
- ensure tasks are challenging but within the learners' capabilities
- give adequate preparation and scaffolding to help them achieve the goal
- give encouragement
- recognise success
- record progress
- attribute value to effort rather than ability

Where to go from here

- Dörnyei (2001) offers the richest collection of motivational strategies to date, specifically selected for the language classroom. Another useful collection of motivational techniques is Alison and Halliwell (2002).

- Dörnyei and Ushioda (2011) provide a comprehensive overview of motivation to learn a foreign language, including the question of demotivation. Dörnyei and Kubanyiova (in press) specifically discuss ways of motivating language learners and language teachers through the use of vision.

- Arnold (1999), Griffiths (2008) and Mercer *et al.* (2012) offer rich collections of accessible papers on various aspects of the psychology of language learning, including motivation.

- Hadfield (1992), Dörnyei and Murphey (2003) and Senior (2006) offer both theoretical and practical material on classroom processes and group dynamics.

- Some useful books relevant to the motivation to learn without a specific language focus include: Anderman and Anderman (2010), Brophy (2004), Gilbert (2002), Ginsberg and Wlodkowski (2000), Good and Brophy (2007), Jones and Jones (2009), McCombs and Miller (2007), Schmuck and Schmuck (2001), Schunk, Pintrich and Meece (2007).

Part IV
From implementation to research

'From implementation to research' presents the final section of the 'research–practice–research' cycle, that is, the stage when a classroom practitioner conducts further explorations on an issue amongst his/her own students in order to:

- improve the quality of the teaching *Class Climate* learning process
- address possible challenges in the classroom
- innovate
- contribute to the advances of theory.

This kind of teacher research has usually been referred to as 'action research' or 'exploratory practice'; for simplicity's sake, we will refer to the wide range of practices that might fall under these categories as 'action research'.

Why do action research?

Action research has been recommended to educators in general as one of the most effective forms of professional development. After all, action research is nothing more than reflecting on interesting or problematic areas in one's teaching in a structured way by looking at some actual information (data). This is something that we often do (or should be doing) anyway – as Keith Richards (2003) has aptly summed up:

> Most ESOL [i.e. EFL/ESL] teachers are natural researchers. We're used to working out the needs of our students, evaluating the effects of particular approaches, spotting things that work or don't work and adjusting our teaching accordingly. Very few teachers approach their work mechanically and nearly all of us reflect on what we do in the classroom.

Besides the general benefits of doing research in the classroom, there are also two specific reasons for deciding to add the 'From implementation to research' part to this book:

(a) It seems to us that the material in this book lends itself to further exploration by classroom practitioners. Vision is an inherently dynamic and situated concept, and the currently available theoretical framework could and should be 'fleshed out' by classroom-oriented investigations (e.g. by case studies of students, evaluations of experimental programmes and lots of actual feedback from students and teachers).

(b) We have come to believe that it is a genuinely exciting and illuminating process to find one's own answers to questions (i.e. to do research), and being engaged in this process can be one of the most self-motivating activities. You would not be reading this book if you were not interested in the topic of motivation, and the suggestions in this chapter might help to extend this topic to your own professional practice.

What is action research?

The term 'action research' was coined by social psychologist Kurt Lewin in the mid-1940s, referring to research as a form of social action. As he famously stated, 'Research that produces nothing but books will not suffice', and thus, right from its genesis, action research was seen as research oriented towards the enhancement of direct practice. As such, it soon found a natural place in the area of education where there has been an ongoing search for ways of creating a close link between research and teaching. If conducted well, action research has the unique capacity to generate a better understanding of an educational environment and to improve the effectiveness of teaching (for recent overviews, see Allwright and Hanks, 2009; Burns, 2010).

Who should do it?

Traditionally only research done by the teachers themselves was considered action research proper. Nowadays the term is also used for various forms of collaboration between teachers and researchers, but the kind of research we are talking about in this section should be initiated or at least partially 'owned' by the teachers (i.e. should involve real collaboration where researchers and teachers participate equally in the research agenda). Thus, we are in full agreement with Anne Burns's (2005) claim that action research 'offers a means for teachers to become agents rather than recipients of knowledge about second language teaching and learning, and thus to contribute towards the building of educational theories of practice'. Accordingly, our answer to the 'Who should do it?' question is that action research should be driven primarily by teachers working in the actual classroom. You may want to invite a researcher as a collaborator (and you would be surprised how many researchers are on the lookout for an appropriate research site and a motivated practitioner-collaborator!), but this should be *your* enterprise.

How?

How can teachers engage in researching vision in the language classroom in a meaningful and viable manner? We suggest that the most straightforward way of finding out how students feel about the role of vision in language learning and the 'visionary activities' that this book contains is by turning to them directly and asking for their feedback and appraisal. The most common method of receiving such feedback is either by means of short questionnaires or by conducting interviews with selected students. We would recommend the latter approach, which is a form of 'qualitative research', since qualitative research has traditionally been seen as an effective way of exploring new, relatively uncharted areas: the role of the vision of the ideal language self in student motivation as well as how this vision can be consciously enhanced are topics that would definitely qualify for this attribute.

Interviewing

Interviews have four broad types, the first three involving a one-to-one format, the fourth a group format:

1. In a *structured interview* the interviewer closely follows a pre-prepared 'interview guide', which contains a list of questions to be covered with every interviewee. This is appropriate if you want to focus on specific issues (e.g. feedback on specific tasks), asking a fair number of students. The interview guide could contain as many as about 15–20 short questions and the answers can be tabulated for the whole group of respondents.

2. The other extreme, the *unstructured interview*, allows maximum flexibility to 'follow' the interviewee into unpredictable directions, with the interviewer primarily assuming a listening role. No detailed interview guide is prepared in advance, although the researcher usually thinks of a few

(1–6) opening questions to elicit the interviewee's story. This is appropriate with talkative students with whom you have a good relationship to ask them about some of the 'big' questions such as the general evaluation of visionary tasks or the self-based approach.

3. *Semi-structured interviews* offer a compromise between the two extremes and would probably be the most appropriate interviewing technique for most projects. Although there is a set of pre-prepared guiding questions and prompts, the format is open-ended and the interviewer is keen to let the interviewee elaborate on certain issues in an exploratory manner even if this means deviating from the questions in the interview guide or changing their order. The interview guide usually focuses on about 3–4 primary areas with a number of specific target topics specified for each. The quality of the interview can be increased by using various 'probes' that use what the interviewee has said as a starting point to go further and to increase the richness and depth of the responses. These probes may include clarification questions ('What do you mean by . . . ?') or the simple but effective technique of taking a salient content word used by the interviewer and ask to elaborate ('You have used the word "freedom" twice – what exactly does it mean to you/do you mean by that . . . ?').

4. *Focus group interviews* involve groups of people (4–6 is a manageable size) discussing a topic, with the interviewer taking on the group leader's role. This format is based on the collective experience of group brainstorming, that is, participants thinking together, inspiring and challenging each other, and reacting to the emerging issues and points. In our experience, students tend to like this format, but you must be careful that the discussion is not dominated by a few 'bigmouths'. You will need an interview guide with about 5–8 broad, open-ended questions accompanied by a few closed-ended ones (i.e. ones that elicit short, specific answers). After all, the strength of this format is the discussion that emerges about a broad topic. You can steer the discussion by using probes, and your body language and gesturing are also effective devices to control the flow and keeping the group focused.

Interview topics and questions

If the goal of your action research is to evaluate and further explore the approach described in this book, then the interviews should focus on the students' general appraisal of the effect of the visionary programmes on their motivation towards learning English, their confidence in mastering and using English, their attitudes towards visualisation, as well as the evaluation of some concrete activities in terms of their perceived usefulness and impact on the students' vision, goals, imagination and emotions. With more open-ended interviews you could also focus on the students' attitudes towards learning English and people living in English-speaking countries, their ideal L2 self, their own dreams and their parents' dreams about how they will use English in the future, any conflicts between their dreams and their parents' dreams and how they try to resolve those conflicts. Here is a list of sample questions that have been used in such studies in the past:

- How much do you like learning English? Do you think you are good at it? Do you like the people who live in English-speaking countries? Would you like to know more about them?

- How do you hope or imagine yourself using English in the future if your dreams come true? Do you have a sense of who you would like to become as an English speaker? Can you imagine a clear situation when you are a successful speaker of English? Who would you be speaking to and where? What would you be using English for? Does this imagination of who you could become in the future motivate your English learning?

- Are you afraid of not becoming a successful user of English? Can you see any specific obstacles that you have to overcome?

- Do you have a sense of what you ought to become as an English speaker/writer? What are your parents' dreams of how you will use English in the future? Do they put pressure on you to study English? Are your dreams for how you want to use English in the future in any way different from those of your parents'? If there is a conflict between your dreams and those of your parents, how do you resolve it?

- Has your image or dream of yourself using English changed over the past few months? Have your reasons for studying English changed?

- How do you feel about the special motivational activities you have done in this course? Do you think using visualisation and imagination activities have helped you? Was it easy for you to visualise in the imagery enhancement practice? What difficulties did you encounter in doing these tasks? What would help/motivate you to participate in them more? Have you any suggestions on how they could be improved?

- How do you evaluate your own progress? Have you improved in any way? Do you feel you have achieved your goals? Do you feel that your English has improved as a result of this course? Do you feel more confident?

- Is there anything else you would like to share about your experiences and thoughts?

Processing the interview data

Whichever interviewing method you choose, our suggestion is that you record the conversation on a digital voice recorder because you simply won't have enough time to take notes during the interviews without losing too much of the content. Professional researchers would then transcribe the recorded texts (which is very time-consuming), but for action research it is usually enough to take notes while you listen to the recordings and mark parts of the data (e.g. by jotting down the counter position or the exact time in seconds) that are particularly useful so that you may be able to go back to them later. With regard to analysing the interview data and reporting the findings, there are several variations depending on your exact purpose (please refer to the recommended books below), but a qualitative report usually contains a balanced mixture of the researcher's insights supported by well-selected extracts from the interviews. In this way both your and your students' voice can be heard.

Further reading

- Zoltán has written a comprehensive research methods book (Dörnyei, 2007) that discusses many procedures to collect, analyse and report both qualitative and quantitative data.

- A user-friendly and insightful guide to qualitative research is Richards (2003), from which we have quoted a short extract above.

- Some other accessible texts addressing research and action research within applied linguistics include Allwright and Hanks (2009), Burns (2010), Mackey and Gass (2005), McKay (2006), Nunan (1992) and Richards, Ross and Seedhouse (2011).

References

Alison, J., and Halliwell, S. (2002). *Challenging classes: focus on pupil behaviour.* London: CILT.

Allwright, D., and Hanks, J. (2009). *The developing language learner: an introduction to exploratory practice.* Basingstoke: Palgrave Macmillan.

Anderman, E. M., and Anderman, L. H. (2010). *Classroom motivation.* Upper Saddle River, NJ: Merrill.

Arnold, J. (ed.) (1999). *Affect in language learning.* Cambridge: Cambridge University Press.

Arnold, J., Puchta, H., and Rinvolucri, M. (2007). *Imagine that! Mental imagery in the EFL classroom.* Cambridge: Cambridge University Press and Helbling.

Berkovits, S. (2005). *Guided imagery: successful techniques to improve school performance and self-esteem.* Duluth, MN: Whole Person Associates.

Brophy, J. (2004). *Motivating students to learn* (2nd edn). Mahwah, NJ: Lawrence Erlbaum.

Burns, A. (2005). Action research. In E. Hinkel (ed.), *Handbook of research in second language teaching and learning* (pp. 241–56). Mahwah, NJ: Lawrence Erlbaum.

Burns, A. (2010). *Doing action research in English language teaching: a guide for practitioners.* New York: Routledge.

Cumming, J. L., and Ste-Marie, D. M. (2001). The cognitive and motivational effects of imagery training: a matter of perspective. *Sport Psychologist*, 15, 276–88.

Dörnyei, Z. (2001). *Motivational strategies in the language classroom.* Cambridge: Cambridge University Press.

Dörnyei, Z. (2005). *The psychology of the language learner: individual differences in second language acquisition.* Mahwah, NJ: Lawrence Erlbaum.

Dörnyei, Z. (2007). *Research methods in applied linguistics: quantitative, qualitative and mixed methodologies.* Oxford: Oxford University Press.

Dörnyei, Z. (2009). The L2 Motivational Self System. In Z. Dörnyei and E. Ushioda (eds), *Motivation, language identity and the L2 self* (pp. 9–42). Bristol: Multilingual Matters.

Dörnyei, Z., and Kubanyiova, M. (in press). *Motivating learners, motivating teachers: building vision in the language classroom.* Cambridge: Cambridge University Press.

Dörnyei, Z., and Murphey, T. (2003). *Group dynamics in the language classroom.* Cambridge: Cambridge University Press.

Dörnyei, Z., and Ushioda, E. (eds) (2009). *Motivation, language identity and the L2 self.* Bristol: Multilingual Matters.

Dörnyei, Z., and Ushioda, E. (2011). *Teaching and researching motivation* (2nd edn). Harlow: Longman.

Dunkel, C., and Kerpelman, J. (eds) (2006). *Possible selves: theory, research, and applications.* New York: Nova Science.

Fezler, W. (1989). *Creative imagery: how to visualize in all five senses.* New York: Simon and Schuster.

Gallwey, T. (1972). *The inner game of tennis.* New York: Bantam Books.

Geiger, John (2006). *The third man factor: surviving the impossible.* New York: Weinstein Books.

Gilbert, I. (2002). *Essential motivation in the classroom.* London: RoutledgeFalmer.

Ginsberg, M. B., and Wlodkowski, R. J. (2000). *Creating highly motivating classrooms for all students: a schoolwide approach to powerful teaching with diverse learners.* San Francisco, CA: Jossey-Bass.

Good, T. L., and Brophy, J. E. (2007). *Looking in classrooms* (10th edn). Upper Saddle River, NJ: Allyn and Bacon.

Gould, D., Damarjian, N., and Greenleaf, C. (2002). Imagery training for peak performance. In J. L. Van Raalte and B. W. Brewer (eds), *Exploring sport and exercise psychology* (2nd edn, pp. 49–74). Washington, DC: American Psychological Association.

Griffiths, C. (ed.) (2008). *Lessons from good language learners*. Cambridge: Cambridge University Press.

Hadfield, J. (1992). *Classroom dynamics*. Oxford: Oxford University Press.

Hall, E., Hall, C., Stradling, P., and Young, D. (2006). *Guided imagery: creative interventions in counselling and psychotherapy*. London: Sage.

Henry, A. (2010). Contexts of possibility in simultaneous language learning: using the L2 Motivational Self System to assess the impact of global English. *Journal of Multilingual and Multicultural Development*, 31(2), 149–62.

Higgins, E. T. (1987). Self-discrepancy: a theory relating self and affect. *Psychological Review*, 94, 319–40.

Johnson, M. (1996). *Slaying the dragon*. London: Piatkus Books.

Jones, V. F., and Jones, L. S. (2009). *Comprehensive classroom management: creating communities of support and solving problems* (9th edn). Upper Saddle River, NJ: Merrill.

Lee, S. J., and Oyserman, D. (2009). Possible selves theory. In E. M. Anderman and L. H. Anderman (eds), *Psychology of classroom learning: an encyclopedia*. Detroit, MI: Macmillan.

Leuner, H., Horn, G., and Klessmann, E. (1983). *Guided affective imagery with children and adolescents*. New York: Plenum.

Lvovich, N. (1997). *The multilingual self*. London: Routledge.

Mackey, A., and Gass, S. M. (2005). *Second language research: methodology and design*. Mahwah, NJ: Lawrence Erlbaum.

Markman, K. D., Klein, W. M. P., and Suhr, J. A. (eds) (2009). *Handbook of imagination and mental simulation*. New York: Psychology Press.

Markus, H. R. (2006). Foreword. In C. Dunkel and J. Kerpelman (eds), *Possible selves: theory, research and applications* (pp. xi–xiv). New York: Nova Science.

Markus, H., and Nurius, P. (1986). Possible selves. *American Psychologist*, 41, 954–69.

McCombs, B. L., and Miller, L. (2007). *Learner-centered classroom practices and assessments: maximizing student motivation, learning, and achievement*. Thousand Oaks, CA: Corwin Press.

McKay, S. L. (2006). *Researching second language classrooms*. Mahwah, NJ: Lawrence Erlbaum.

Mercer, S., Ryan, S., and Williams, M. (eds) (2012). *Psychology for language learning: insights from research, theory and practice*. Basingstoke: Palgrave Macmillan.

Morris, T., Spittle, M., and Watt, A. P. (2005). *Imagery in sport*. Champaign, IL: Human Kinetics.

Murray, G., Gao, X., and Lamb, T. (eds) (2011). *Identity, motivation and autonomy in language learning*. Bristol: Multilingual Matters.

Norton, B. (2000). *Identity and language learning: social processes and educational practice*. Harlow: Pearson.

Nunan, D. (1992). *Research methods in language learning*. Cambridge: Cambridge University Press.

Oyserman, D., and James, L. (2009). Possible selves: from content to process. In K. Markman, W. M. P. Klein and J. A. Suhr (eds), *The handbook of imagination and mental stimulation* (pp. 373–94). New York: Psychology Press.

Oyserman, D., and Markus, H. R. (1990). Possible selves and delinquency. *Journal of Personality and Social Psychology*, 59, 112–25.

Pavlenko, A., and Blackledge, A. (eds) (2004). *Negotiation of identities in multilingual contexts*. Clevedon: Multilingual Matters.

Richards, K. (2003). *Qualitative inquiry in TESOL*. Basingstoke: Palgrave Macmillan.

Richards, K., Ross, S. J., and Seedhouse, P. (2011). *Research methods for applied language studies: an advanced resource book for students*. London: Routledge.

Schmuck, R. A., and Schmuck, P. A. (2001). *Group processes in the classroom* (8th edn). Boston, MA: McGraw-Hill.

Schunk, D. H., Pintrich, P. R., and Meece, J. (2007). *Motivation in education: theory, research, and applications* (3rd edn). Upper Saddle River, NJ: Merrill.

Segal, H. G. (2006). Possible selves, fantasy distortion, and the anticipated life history: exploring the role of imagination in social cognition. In C. Dunkel and J. Kerpelman (eds), *Possible selves: theory, research and applications* (pp. 79–96). New York: Nova Science.

Senior, R. M. (2006). *The experience of language teaching*. Cambridge: Cambridge University Press.

Singer, J. L. (2006). *Imagery in psychotherapy.* Washington, DC: American Psychological Association.

Taylor, S. E., Pham, L. B., Rivkin, I. D., and Armor, D. A. (1998). Harnessing the imagination: mental simulation, self-regulation, and coping. *American Psychologist*, 53(4), 429–39.